OPTIONS TRADING

*Mastering the Art of Options Trading
for Financial Success
(2023 Guide for Beginners)*

Lee kirk

Table of Contents

CHAPTER 1

OPTIONS: THE FUNDAMENTALS

WHAT EXACTLY IS AN OPTION?

An option is essentially a contract on the underlying shares of stock. It is an agreement to swap shares at a certain price over a set period of time (they may be purchased or sold). The first thing you should know about choices is the following.

Why would someone go into options trading in the first place? Most individuals enter options trading with the intention of profiting from the options themselves. And most readers of this book will most likely fit that description. But, in order to properly appreciate what you're doing, you must first understand why alternatives exist in the first place. There are probably three basic reasons why stock options exist.

The first reason is that it enables those who own stock to earn money from their investment regularly. As a result, it might serve as an alternative to or supplement dividend income. As we will see later, if you possess at least 100 shares of any stock, this is a possibility. Then, in general, you may sell options against the stock and generate cash over time periods ranging from a week to a month.

Obviously, such a move involves some risk, but individuals will take such positions when the relative risk is modest.

The second reason individuals invest in options is because they provide protection against a stock's downfall. So, once again, an option entails being able to trade shares of stock at a predetermined price determined at the time the contract is formed. One sort of contract enables the buyer to acquire stock, while the other permits the buyer to sell stock. This enables customers who possess a big number of shares to buy something that protects their investment by allowing them to sell the shares at a predetermined price if their stock falls by a substantial amount on the market. As a result, the premise is identical to paying insurance premiums.

It's unknown how many people really utilize this, but it's one of the reasons choices exist. This would operate by paying someone a premium to obtain the right to sell your shares to them at a preset price over a certain period of time. If the share price falls much below that level, you will still be able to sell your shares and escape the market's massive losses.

The third reason for the existence of options, in my opinion, is that it allows individuals to create agreements to acquire shares of stock at attractive prices that aren't always accessible on the market. As a result, there is some guesswork here. But suppose a certain stock you're interested in is priced at $100 per share. Furthermore, pretend that investors are highly enthusiastic about the stock and anticipate it to skyrocket in the following weeks. Perhaps it's earnings season.

During results season, stocks may fluctuate dramatically. However, nobody knows whether the stock will rise or fall or how much it will change before the results call. An options contract might enable someone to speculate and build up a scenario in which they could benefit from a large upward increase without actually investing in the stock.

The Benefits of Option Trading

Investors may benefit greatly from options trading. Essentially, it is an investment that allows people with the funds to enter into an income-generating endeavor. The benefits of options trading are many and should entice individuals to enter the industry of trading stocks, selling and buying assets, and earning income.

The first is this venture's potential to assist in risk management while investing in stocks and securities. They can protect you from incurring investment losses. This is due to the fact that investing in stocks and shares typically entails risks in the value of the shares.

This depreciation may reduce income and, in certain cases, reduce the value of shares held. However, options marketing ensures that one is hedged against such uncertainties and also assures that one may generate value from the selling of shares.

Options trading is also useful in that it gives someone time to determine whether or not to acquire anything. This is a special benefit of call options. The contract normally includes a term during which a person contemplates exercising implied rights. Before deciding whether or not to acquire the shares, the individual researches the market and its performance and has the opportunity to comprehend his financial status. As a result, well-thought-out investment judgments are made. It always comes with increased preparation to deal with the repercussions of one's actions. This assists in breaking the habit of making trading choices based on whims, which may subsequently lead to tension and stress when market forces come into play.

Leverage

Leverage is a particularly favorable characteristic of options trading that individuals attempt to use in order to engage in the securities market. When using leverage, one must make lesser outlay with the hope of reaping larger gains. This motivates individuals who lack the funds to invest in underlying assets or shares to find another avenue to invest and earn rewards. One of the most essential aspects of leverage is that one generally receives returns on the underlying assets or shares while not having to pay the entire cost of the shares.

The concept of leverage includes the benefit of diversity.

This is accomplished by establishing a portfolio without making large initial investments. This diversity may then provide a stream of investment channels, which in turn can lead to profits, boosting one's earnings. When one purchase call options that are placed back on the shares held, this revenue may sometimes exceed dividends. This additional revenue may even come from shares that were obtained via a loan arrangement. Option premiums also arrive ahead of trading operations, buffering one from potential losses.

What exactly is an option contract?

When you choose to work with an options contract, you will be granted a variety of privileges. Each contract you choose to deal with will have the following information:

The sort of choice you're considering. This is a call option or a put option.

The option contains the underlying security.

dealing with options has the advantage of allowing you to choose whether or not to execute them, which reduces the risk of dealing with them somewhat. If the market does not perform as you expected, you simply let the expiry date pass and do nothing. You will lose the original payment, but you will not lose as much money as you would if you were obliged to execute a terrible decision.

When it comes to day trading, the expiry date of the option should be as short as possible. Even though options for other trading techniques might last days, weeks, or even months, you must still complete both the buy and sell of the option and its underlying asset on the same day. Make sure to choose an expiry date that corresponds to the day trading you are conducting.

\

Option Contract Components

There are many standardized components of option contracting that make options trading easier. These components define how options trading binds the parties involved and illustrate how profits may be created if market dynamics are favorable. Options trading includes the following components:

- Underlying securities

- Contract size

- Expiration date

- Exercise pricing

Subsidiary securities

Options traded on the market only apply to certain assets. These assets are known as underlying securities. In certain cases, the term shares may be used for the word shares.

Companies offer the asset against which the option operators list options. ASX is one options trading market operator that has played an important role in the listing of underlying securities.

The phrase option classes refer to the listing of puts and calls as options on the same asset. As an example, consider when puts and calls are applied to the shares of a leasing company. This does not take into account the contract conditions in terms of the fixed price or the expiration length of the call and put contracts. For the advantage of investors, an options trading operator generally gives a list of possible classes.

Size of the Contract

The market standardizes the size of the option contract on the ASX options trading platform at 100 underlying equities. As a result, one option contract equals 100 underlying shares. Changes may occur only when reorganization occurs on the original outlay of the underlying share or capital therein. Index options typically lock in the contract's value at a certain dollar rate.

Day of expiry

Options are time-limited and have a shelf life. The platform operator establishes expiration dates that must be followed. These deadlines are often strict, and once they pass, the rights under a contract in a certain class of unexercised options are lost. The final trading date is often the last day of a contract's life period. Options on shares that will expire in June of 2020 have their final trading day on a Thursday that is prior to the month's last Friday. Those that expire after June 2020 have their expiration date on the third Thursday of the month. For index choices. Expiries occur on the third

Thursday of the month in which the option was written. These dates, however, may be altered by the options platform operator if there is a cause for doing so.

Platform operators have provided additional short-term choices for several underlying in recent years. Some are done weekly, while others are done every two weeks. These have the relevant weekly or biweekly expiration dates. When an option's life span expires, the operators set new deadlines. However, all kinds of options have expiry dates that correspond to financial calendar quarters.

CHAPTER 2

WHAT AFFECTS OPTION PRICES?

When it comes to options trading, pricing is a complicated matter. Not only is the price of an option determined by the asset's value, but other external variables also have a role.x

As an options trader, you want to make the most of your efforts in order to benefit. Learning how to estimate the pricing you should pay for options is one of the most fundamental techniques to guarantee that your return is as high as possible. You do not want to be taken advantage of by paying greater premiums than necessary. Several variables influence the pricing of options. Each will be mentioned below.

The Asset's Market Value

The impact on option pricing is simple. If the value of this asset falls, executing the option to sell becomes more valuable, while exercising the option to purchase gets less lucrative.

On the other hand, if the value rises, the right to sell it becomes less attractive, but the right to acquire it gets more enticing.

The Intrinsic Worth

This sum reflects two values when an options trader pays a premium. The premium is made up of the intrinsic value of the option, which is its present value, and the potential rise in value that this option may receive through time. The potential rise over time is referred to as the time value.

We're talking about inherent worth. The intrinsic value is the amount of money that the option is now worth. It shows what the buyer would get if he or she opted to exercise the option right now.

Intrinsic value is computed by subtracting the current price of an asset from the strike price of an option. An option must be out of money in order to have an inherent value of zero. As a consequence, the buyer would decline to exercise the option since doing so would result in a loss. The conventional technique here is to let the option lapse so that no payment is paid. As a consequence, the buyer receives nothing from the inherent value.

In order for a buyer to be in the money, the intrinsic value must be larger than the premium to enhance the option's value. This puts the buyer in a position to benefit. The intrinsic value of in-the-money call and put options is computed significantly differently. The following are the formulas:

The Time Worthiness

This value is the amount an investor is prepared to give to an option's premium in addition to the intrinsic value. This willingness derives from the notion that an option's value will rise before its expiry date. Typically, an investor will only put up this additional money if the option expires in a few months. In a few days, the value of an option would alter little to nothing.

The time value is computed by subtracting the intrinsic value of an option from the premium. The formula is as follows:

Time Value = Option Premium - Intrinsic Value

As a result, the total price of an option premium is calculated as follows:

Option Premium = Intrinsic Value + Time Value

If a trader decides to acquire an option, both temporal value and intrinsic value might assist them grasp the worth of what they are paying for.

While the intrinsic value indicates the value of the option if the buyer exercises it now, the temporal value provides the potential future value before or on the expiry date.

These two variables are significant because they assist traders in determining the risk vs benefit of selecting an option.

Volatility

This indicates the likelihood of a price shift occurring in the financial market over a certain period of time. If a financial market is nonvolatile, prices move extremely slowly or stay completely unaltered over a certain period of time. Volatile markets, on the other hand, feature rapidly fluctuating prices over short time periods.

Options traders might take advantage of a financial market's volatility to increase the return on their investment in the future. Options traders often avoid nonvolatile financial markets since they frequently signify that no possible profit is available to the trader. As a result, even while volatility increases the risk of option trading, options traders thrive on it. As a consequence, an options trader must understand how to accurately analyze the financial market in order to determine which options are likely to offer the largest profits. This competence is gained through experience, ongoing learning, and staying current on financial market events.

Many variables influence the volatility of a financial market. Politics, the national economy, and news stories are among these causes. To maximize profit from turbulent markets, options traders often choose one of two tactics. They are known as the straddle and strangle strategies.

Rates of Interest

The word interest rates are well-known to most people. Mortgages, bank accounts, and other financial products all have interest rates. Interest rates as they apply to options trading vary somewhat from the conventional versions.

The interest rate is defined as a percentage of a certain rate for the usage of money loaned over time. This option's interest rate has various implications on the call and put options. Call option premiums climb when interest rates rise and decrease when interest rates fall. On put options, the impact is the inverse. Put option premiums decrease when interest rates increase and climb when interest rates fall. Interest rates impact the temporal value of options regardless of their type!

In your study of options trading, you will come across the phrase risk-free interest rate many times. This is defined as the return on an investment with no capital loss. This is a deceptive word since all investments, no matter how little, include some element of risk. This is more of a parameter in option pricing models like the Black-Scholes Model that determines the premium that should be paid.

Dividends

Dividends are payments made from a company's profits over a certain time period. A company's board of directors must determine and oversee this distribution. It is distributed to a certain group of stockholders. Dividends may be issued in the form of cash, stock shares, or other property. Dividends are also paid out by exchange-traded funds and mutual funds.

Options do not pay dividends in the context of options trading.

However, the linked assets tied to that option may have them, and therefore the options trader may earn those dividends if he or she exercises the option and acquires ownership of those specific assets. While the availability of dividends from the underlying asset may impact both calls and put options, the effect on the kinds of options varies greatly. While the existence of dividends makes call options less costly owing to the expectation of a price decline, it makes put options more expensive since the price will be reduced by the dividend amount.

Models of Option Pricing

To compute the value of an option, option pricing theory employs all of the factors described above. It is a tool that enables trainers to get an assessment of an option's fair value as they implement various techniques to enhance profitability. Fortunately, traders may utilize models to execute option pricing methods to their benefit.

The following are three regularly used pricing models for option values:

The Black-Scholes Equation

Model of Binomial Option Pricing

Simulations using the Monte-Carlo method

The Black Scholes Equation

This pricing model, often known as the Black-Scholes-Merton (BSM) model, was awarded the Nobel Prize in Economics for its efficacy.

In 1973, three economists, Fischer Black, Robert Merton, and Myron Scholes, created it. This is a mathematical approach that has a large effect on current option pricing. It was first used to price European options (meaning the option may only be exercised on the expiry date). The pricing model distinguishes options from gambling by calculating the option premium to be paid in a rational way. It computes the investor's expected return on investment minus the amount paid.

Because this is generally used to determine a European call option, the method for calculating it is as follows:

Call Option Premium = SN(d1) - Xe - rt N(d2).

The letter symbols in this equation stand for:

S stands for the current asset price.

N denotes a normal distribution.

X is the strike price, while r is the risk-free interest rate.

t - maturity time

While this pricing mechanism is excellent, it has certain drawbacks. One of these disadvantages is that it implies that variables like volatility and risk-free interest would stay constant, which is not the case. It also does not account for any additional expenses associated with setting up the option.

Model of Binomial Option Pricing

This pricing technique, which is more typically used to establish prices for American options, was devised in 1979. Even though the Black Scholes Model is popular, this model is more often employed in practice since it is more intuitive. This pricing method assumes two alternative outcomes: one in which the result goes up and one in which the outcome moves down.

This approach varies from the Black Scholes Model in that it allows for multiple period computations, while the Black Scholes Model does not. This advantage provides a multi-period picture, which is highly useful for options traders.

Binomial trees are used in this methodology to determine option pricing.

These are diagrams with a core formula branching out in two directions. This branching is what gives this pricing method its famed multi-period perspective.

The following assumptions are made in order for this pricing system to work:

The connected asset has two alternative prices, thus the name of the pricing system. Bi signifies "two."

The asset's price may go up or down in either direction.

There are no dividends payable on the asset.

The interest rate remains constant during the option's life.

There are no risks associated with this transaction.

There are no additional expenses connected with this choice.

Those assumptions, like the Black Scholes Model, clearly have certain limitations. Nonetheless, the pricing mechanism is very beneficial in evaluating American options since such options may be exercised at any moment until the expiry date.

Simulations using Monte Carlo methods

This approach, which is used in a variety of sectors including science, engineering, and finance, enables the options trader to examine different possibilities owing to the participation of random elements. Unlike the other two pricing models, it allows for the consideration of risk and unpredictability. This is why it is also known as multiple probability simulation.

A Final Thought on Pricing

I went into such detail on pricing choices because I want you to understand that everything about options, even down to the premiums paid, deserves careful thought. This must be a fair transaction for all parties involved, and premium pricing must reflect this fairness. When examining the options premium, remember to go below the surface level to verify the fairness and that you are earning the profit that you need from the transaction.

CHAPTER 3

THE TRADER'S MINDSET

Someone who is new to the notion of trading options will only be concerned with generating money. When their traders are winning, they will rejoice, and they will disregard the transactions that are losing money. This may come naturally to them, but it is a horrible idea. To become a long-term and successful trader, you must not only pay attention when the trades are going your way, but you must also comprehend why some of your transactions lose money. When you do this, it becomes much simpler to limit the number of failed transactions since you understand what to avoid in general.

No matter how long you've been in the market, you'll sometimes make winning transactions in options, and other times you'll make losing ones. As you spend more experience trading options, you will improve your ability to understand the market and apply the methods correctly.

However, there will be situations when the deals do not go as planned.

Trading psychology refers to the mental state and emotions that influence the success or failure of options trading. It indicates the component of your personality that influences your choices when presented with a deal. The mentality of a trader is as important as experience, education, and abilities in deciding your success as a trader.

When you decide to start trading options, you must understand the concepts of risk-taking and discipline, which govern the execution of each deal.

Greed and fear are the two most frequent emotions, followed by regret and hope.

We relate trading psychology with certain actions and emotions that are often the drivers for choices. Fear and greed are two of the most typical emotions that any trader will encounter.

Fear

Fear is one of the worst feelings that you may have at any one moment. Checking your newspaper one day, you read about a severe selloff, and the next thing you know, you're trying to figure out what to do next, even if it's not the best course of action at the moment.

Many investors believe they know what will happen in the next few days, which gives them a high level of confidence in the trade's conclusion. As a result, investors enter the transaction at either too high or too low a level, causing them to respond emotionally.

As the trader places a lot of faith in a single deal, the degree of dread rises, and doubt and caution take over.

dread is a component of every trader, yet good traders can handle their dread. There are different sorts of worries that you may encounter; here are a few examples:

The Fear of Failure

Have you ever started a transaction and all you could think about was the possibility of losing? The fear of losing makes it difficult to execute the ideal plan or enter or quit a strategy at the appropriate moment.

As a trader, you understand the importance of making choices when the strategy tells you to. When fear guides you, your level of confidence lowers, and you lack the capacity to execute the plan correctly and on time. When a plan fails, you lose faith in both your ability and the approach.

When you lose faith in many of your tactics, you have analysis paralysis, which means you are unable to act on any choice you make. Making a move becomes very difficult.

When you can't pull the trigger, all you can think about is avoiding the agony of losing, even when you need to go on.

No trader enjoys losing, but even the greatest traders may experience losses from time to time. The aim is for them to make more successful transactions in order to remain in the game.

When you worry excessively, you get sidetracked from your execution process and instead concentrate on the outcomes.

Accepting losses is necessary to lessen trading anxiety. The possibility of losing or profiting is 50/50, and you must accept this reality before proceeding with a transaction, whether it is a sell or a buy indication.

Afraid about a Positive Trend Negative Thinking (and vice versa)

Many traders like to take rapid gains and then let their losses run. Many traders want to feel like they've earned some money for the day, so they opt for a fast profit to give themselves the winning sensation.

So, what should you do in its place? You should follow the crowd.

When you detect a trend beginning, it is best to stick with it until you get an indication that the trend is going to reverse. Only then do you leave this situation?

To grasp this notion, you must first comprehend the market's history. History is excellent at demonstrating how times change and trends may go either way. Remember that no one knows when a trend will begin or stop; all you have to do is wait for the indication.

The Panic of Missing Out

People who mistrust the ability of trade to succeed exist for every transaction. After you make the deal, you will be confronted with a slew of critics who will cast doubt on the whole operation and leave you questioning whether or not to abandon the approach.

This concern is also defined by greed, since you aren't operating on the assumption of making a profitable transaction, but rather that the security is growing without you getting a piece of the pie.

This worry is frequently based on the knowledge that there is a trend that you missed and might have profited from.

This anxiety has a drawback in that it causes you to disregard any possible risks involved with the transaction and instead believe that you have the ability to profit since others have benefitted from the activity.

Fear of Making a Mistake

Many traders place so much importance on being correct that they lose sight of the fact that they are running a company. They also fail to see that being successful is all about understanding the trend and how it influences their participation.

When you use the optimal timing technique, you get a lot of good outcomes in a short period of time.

The weird need to constantly be right rather than concentrate on generating money is a large part of your ego, and in order to remain on the correct track, you must trade without your ego for a while.

If you approach trading with a perfectionist mindset, you will be chasing failure since you will encounter a lot of losses. Perfectionists do not handle defeats well, which leads to terror.

Ways to Overcome Trading Fear

As you can see, fear may clearly result in losses. So, how can you overcome this fear and achieve success?

Learn

You must discover a means to acquire information so that you can make judgments. When you know all there is to know about options, you will know what to purchase and when to sell, as well as which ones to monitor. You are then more confident in making sound judgments.

Consider the larger picture.

You should constantly review your decisions and examine what you have won or lost so far before taking any action. Understanding your errors allows you to make better judgments in the future.

Begin Small

Many traders who believe in fear have lost a lot of money in the past. They placed a lot of money on the line and lost, which made them afraid to conduct additional deals. Begin with little funds to avoid putting yourself in too much danger. As you gain confidence, you may invest in bigger quantities for more rewards.

Use the Proper Strategy

Having the appropriate trading strategy makes it simple to execute winning deals. Examine numerous options trading techniques to see which one is best for your position and talents.

Many tactics may help you succeed, while others may confuse you. If you have a plan that isn't producing the desired results, alter it over time to meet your objectives. Refine it till you are satisfied with its performance.

Keep it simple.

When you have a basic and obvious approach, you are less likely to lose confidence along the road since you know what to anticipate.

Furthermore, the simpler the technique, the quicker any flaws will be identified.

Don't be hesitant.

Sometimes you have to plunge into the fight even if you aren't sure how it works. You will learn more about the trade after you start taking action.

However, while engaging in any commerce, you must always be prepared.

The more prepared you are, the simpler it will be to conduct effective deals.

Never Give Up

Things may not always go the way you expect them to. Remember that errors are meant to teach you lessons that will help you become a better trader. When you lose, take the time to figure out what went wrong and then fix it before trying again.

Greed

This refers to a selfish desire to get more money from a deal than you need. When the drive to get more than you can normally make takes over your decision-making process, you are setting yourself up for failure.

Greed is seen to be more harmful than fear. Yes, fear might cause you to lose transactions, but the good news is that you get to keep your cash. Greed, on the other hand, causes you to spend your money quicker than you can return it. It forces you to act when you should not be acting.

Greed Can Be Dangerous

Greed causes people to behave irrationally. Overtrading, overleveraging, holding positions for too long, or chasing other markets are all examples of irrational trading behavior.

The more your greed, the dumber your actions are. If you reach a point when greed overpowers common sense, you've gone too far.

When you are greedy, you wind up risking much more than you can manage, and you end up losing. You also have excessive market expectations, giving the impression that you are just interested in money.

Greed causes you to trade early and without any understanding of the options trading market.

When you are greedy, your judgment is clouded, and you do not consider any bad implications that may follow from particular actions.

Many traders who were too greedy gave up after making this error during the early trading session.

How to Get Rid of Greed

To combat greed, like with any other trading activity, a lot of work is required. It may not be simple since we are discussing human emotions, but it is achievable.

To begin, you must understand that not every decision you make will be correct at all times. There may be occasions when you will make the wrong decision and end up losing money. At times, you will completely miss the ideal plan and fail to advance.

Second, you must acknowledge that the market is much larger than you.

You will accept and make errors as a result of doing so.

CHAPTER 4

FUNDAMENTALS

WHAT IS A COVERED CALL PURCHASE?

Purchasing a covered call entails purchasing a stock at a predetermined price. As an example, suppose you want to acquire some IBM shares. Instead of writing to purchase it at a set price, you buy it from the trader when the stock falls below a given threshold.

Assume the IBM stock is now trading at $45 per share. You purchase a covered call stating that the stock would be sold at $40 per share. So, the stock rises to $47, and you buy it for $40, resulting in a $700 savings on the stock price. If it falls below $39, you will be unable to exercise this option, and you will lose the premium, whatever it may be.

Buying and selling covered calls

Most beginners prefer to dangle their toes in the treacherous waters of options trading by selling covered calls.

It's the most basic level of options trading, and although it's not the most exciting, it's a wonderful way to get your feet wet before going on to more intricate techniques.

In the long run, selling covered calls is likely to be part of your options strategy. Many traders utilize it as a consistent source of revenue - a prudent basis for their accounts.

A third advantage of beginning with covered calls is that it contains the bulk of the information and approach that you will employ as an options trader, making it an excellent training ground.

Using this approach, you will sell the right to purchase underlying stocks that you hold. A "covered" call is so named because you own the shares and hence have the sale covered.

Before you can begin, you must first possess at least 100 shares or one stock. By putting an option on those shares, you provide purchasers the opportunity to purchase them before the expiry date if the share price reaches your strike price.

You will get the premium if a buyer takes advantage of your offer. That is yours to keep; whether the strike price is reached and the buyer exercises their right or not, you will never have to return it. That is your motivation for selling covered calls: the consistent inflow of income from premiums.

It's also a smart approach to sell your stock; savvy traders would use this strategy to cleanse their portfolio of shares they no longer desire to possess. In the meanwhile, there are benefits to holding that stock. If the price rises, you may get dividends as well as capital gains (the difference between the current price and the higher price at the time of selling) when the deadline approaches.

Selling Covered Calls Strategy

We've gone through the procedure, but what about the strategy?

We looked at the fundamentals of that technique, but any experienced trader knows that there is always more to an option than meets the eye.

There are several things that you will want to keep in mind as you improve your knowledge and design your own, particular plan. Every trader has a distinct perspective on what works and what doesn't - there are several methods to make selling a covered call profitable, but you'll probably favor one or two tactics.

We'll look at those aspects in further depth now to help you as you go deeper into the covered call:

The Market Situation: You are probably aware that stock and share traders are pleased in a bull market and unhappy in a down market. You may also be aware that such traders despise a flat market since there is little activity and little opportunity for large gains. The reverse is true for you, as a covered call seller. I strongly advise waiting for the market to briefly flatten before engaging in a flurry of covered call sales. This is because you're only concerned with tiny fluctuations in your share prices; if they soar, you'll lose more money on your contract. There is also less risk of the market bottoming out and your stock values collapsing at the same moment, which would be troublesome.

Your underpinning stock is: Nothing is more critical to your long-term success than selecting the appropriate companies to invest in in the first place. I cannot emphasize enough how important it is to choose equities that go up slowly. You don't want equities that rise and fall fast, particularly if you're a newbie since they have a propensity of making unexpected changes that might derail your approach. If they fall too much, you risk losing a lot of money on the sale; if they rise too far, you risk losing the money you might have gained if you'd sold them at that price.

Always remember that the premium is your assured profit. Whatever else happens, you're going to get that money. You'll be able to determine the real profit you'll earn on that premium after you add in the cost of listing the option and any fee you'll forfeit to your broker. Set a minimum premium - a figure you believe is sufficient to create a profit you'll be comfortable with, assuming it's the only profit you earn. When it comes time to pick the strike price, you'll most likely alter this base amount up or down depending on what you believe the underlying stock will do before the expiry date.

The Date of Expiration: There's a reason why premiums on covered calls rise as the expiry date approaches. It's because, much like the weather predictions we all despise on a daily basis, predicting what will happen to a share price becomes more difficult as time passes. Remember that your money will be locked up until the expiry date, thus the premium will rise to compensate for that sacrifice. Most investors feel that a time frame of one to three months is ideal.

The Strike Price: You would believe that the strike price you select should be based on what you are comfortable with as the seller, but this is not the case. You want to find a striking price that your customer is comfortable with, or else they will not purchase. This, in turn, will be determined by the expiry date you choose, as well as the premium you want and how stable or volatile the underlying stock is.

With all of these considerations, you're probably beginning to understand that there is no one "correct decision" when it comes to selling covered calls. It will take some time and effort to discover which ones work best for you.

It's also worth noting that your approach will most likely vary as you acquire experience. The more options you sell, the more you will find new and improved methods to profit from the market. For the time being, I advise you to be cautious in your approach and understand that selling covered options will not make you rich - but it will help you expand the seed money you have available to do so.

Discovering the Best Stock and Strike Price for a Covered Call

So, how do you go about finding the correct stock for this? Again, you want to pick a company that has enough volatility to get to the price that you want it to be, pays fair dividends, and is in a field that will be there for a long time.

DSL is one that is now booming. You could believe it won't perform as well, yet it still has an outstanding quantity of dividends. That is, if you can locate equities that are being sold, have the potential to alter the game for the better in the future, and are also worth investing in, you should do so.

You should seek a stock that you believe you can readily get. If there are a lot of open positions on the stock, I recommend taking your time and putting effort into it. You'd be surprised at how much of a difference it can make.

How to Purchase a Profitable Covered Call

So, how do you acquire a covered call and a stock that you wish to own? How do you go about it? The solution is straightforward.

First, look at the stock you want to purchase, the shares, and how much you'll have to spend, particularly in comparison to the premiums.

So, let's assume you want to purchase shares in Ford because, hey, Ford is introducing a new engine and automobile set, and you believe the price will rise. You may do the same with Apple since there are reports that the MacBook Pro 2019 will be released next month or something. Many individuals like jumping on Apple-covered calls immediately before the unveiling of new iPhones. So, you go into your account and search for a stock with a price in the range you choose. The strike price should be reasonable, such as 14 dollars per share for 100 shares. Now that you're inside, you choose the call that you want to purchase, and maybe you select that call choice and check to see how many days this will last. You should then choose the option to receive this call.

If you right-click there, you can pick what you want to do with the covered stock and whether or not you want a contract for this one. You may be led to a website to fill out the information at this point, and from there, you should check to see what your cost base is going to be and how much you're going to spend. You should seek a reasonable price for the shares and avoid allowing them to fall too much.

If the stock is declining in value, do not buy it. That's a sinking ship, and you may bid farewell to it. However, after you pick this, you will begin to look at the stock, and whenever you find that the shares are trading at a higher price than what you paid for the covered call, you may log in and opt to execute it.

Once you've exercised it, the investor is compelled to sell you the option, and you may now purchase the covered call option you desire at the price that is specified.

Now consider the inverse. Assume you didn't see the patterns altering all that much, and the stock got stagnant.

Unfortunately, the longer you wait, the less variation there will be in the stock. Your objective is to get out of there as quickly as possible. The issue is that the stock will remain in that range over time.

You want to invest as soon as you realize there will be a significant shift.

So, yeah, just before the Apple announcement, the stock will be excellent, and you can cash in on that option right away. But suppose it's been a slow month and you haven't done anything with it. The investor from whom you purchased it will get it.

CHAPTER 5

IN THE MONEY, OUT OF THE MONEY

IN THE MONEY

Before we get there, let's go over some key market terms. The first phrase we must learn is "in the money." Calls are simpler to grasp since if you are not an experienced market trader, you are not accustomed to thinking in terms of shorting stocks. The majority of individuals want stock prices to grow. As you learn more about options trading, you'll realize that it's not always the ideal alternative. Calls, on the other hand, have an inherent appeal to that basic belief, cognitive process, and desire.

A call option is called in the money when the market price of a particular stock exceeds the option's average strike price. So, if you have a $75 strike price option and the company is selling at $80 per share, it is in the money. In summary, call options that are in the money are much more valuable than those that are not.

We may use the choices calculator to see what the changes are.

So, I've created a fictitious stock that trades at $80 per share. We will take into account a 14-day option. For the record, the implied volatility is 16%, and the risk-free rate is 0.3% (more on that in a moment).

With the strike price set at $75, the option (in this instance a call) is priced at $5.03. Remember that the total price of the option would be $503 for a single share.

Consider another option that has all of the same features but has a strike price of $70. This option costs $10.01 to purchase, or $1001 to sell. The option with a strike price of $70 is likewise profitable, but it is more profitable than the option with a strike price of $75. Another way to communicate this idea is that it is deeper in the money.

The option is considered to be at the money if the share price is precisely equal to the strike price. In the actual world, the chances of an option being precisely at the money are minimal, but they may be quite near. These options are interesting because if the stock price rises over the strike price, the option's value may skyrocket by a considerable margin.

The likelihood of the share price going above the strike price is quite high for a call option. Using a strike price of $75 as an example, the option would cost $0.92 (you would have to spend $92 to acquire the option). If the share price climbs to $76 later that day, the call price will rise to $1.53.

This kind of price movement exemplifies why individuals are drawn to trading options. If you sold right then and there, you'd make $61 on each option contract.

Out of Pocket

When the strike price is more than the market share price, the option is said to be out of the money.

Options do not have to be in the money to be profitable.

Out-of-the-money options may also be profitable depending on the direction of price movement. We can see this with call choices.

If the stock price rises, the price of out-of-the-money calls will climb as well. So, we'll create a similar situation in which there are 14 days till option expiry, but this time the strike price is $77. If the share price is $75, which is less than the strike, the option is worthless.

You may potentially earn a significant profit if the share price climbs during the following several days. The advantage of out-of-pocket choices is that they are quite inexpensive.

In our case, the $77 strike would cost $0.27 ($27 to purchase).

Assume that the share price climbs to $76.50 two days later. The option is still unprofitable. However, the option's price will climb when the share price rises. It turns out that under these criteria, the option would cost $0.66 at that time. That implies you could sell it for $66 after purchasing it for $27 only two days before.

Many experts advise against trading out-of-the-money options.

However, they continue to be a terrific option for those who don't have a lot of money to start producing money. This can work if the underlying stock's price moves significantly and you only hold the option for a few days. If there is a lot of activity in a single day, you may really earn a lot of money.

Consider a viable alternative for Apple. Consider a $220 strike price option that expires in 16 days. Apple was trading at $192.50 per share at the start of the session. At the time, the call option was priced at $0.08, which meant that you could have bought each option's contract for just $8. Apple's stock price increased to $195.76 later in the morning. The price of the $200 strike price option fell to $0.16 (or $16 for all 100 shares). As a result, we would have the potential to double our money, and to make it more substantial, you may purchase numerous options at the same time. Always keep an eye on the liquidity. The volume for the option is 102, while the open interest is 269. That would be sufficient liquidity to terminate the trade in a timely manner.

Remember that if an option expires out of the money, it is likewise worthless (it "expires worthless"). This is also true for the financial possibilities. If the option is in the money when it expires, the option price is (share price - strike price).

CHAPTER 6

TAKING THE NEXT STEP IN TRADING WITH CALLS

A call option contract grants the holder the right to purchase 100 shares of stock (per contract) at a set strike price that does not fluctuate regardless of the actual market cost of capital. A call alternative contract can look like this:

1 PKT Dec 40 Call with a $500 premium. PKT is the stock on which you are purchasing the agreement. One means one alternative contract addressing 100 PKT offers. The basic principle and how-to-trade call options in this model is that you pay $500, which is 100% at risk if you don't do anything with the agreement before December, but you retain the right to purchase 100 offers of the stock at 40. As a result, if PKT rises to 60. You may rehearse the agreement by purchasing 100 offers at 40. When you swiftly sell the stock on the open market, you will realize a gain of 20 points, or $2000. You paid a $500 premium, thus your total net gain in this options trading strategy would be $1500. So, whether you are long or have gotten a call option, you normally need the market to climb.

Trading Strategy vs. Premium Practice and Understanding

The extraordinary will rise as the market on the first stock rises using call options. Buyer requests will be increased. This rise in premiums encourages the financial advisor to trade the option on the market for a profit. So, you are repurchasing the agreement rather than practicing it. The difference between the superior you paid and the superior it was sold for will be to your advantage. The benefit for persons attempting to figure out how to trade options or get acquainted with the nuts and bolts of a trading technique is that you don't have to acquire a stock outright to benefit from its increase using calls.

Why Should You Invest in Call Options?

When you are optimistic about a stock, you purchase a call option. In other words, you purchase a call option when you predict the underlying stock's price to climb. In theory, if you purchase a call option, you are intending to purchase shares of stock at the strike price, which you anticipate will be lower than the market price at some time.

Assume a stock is trading at $99 per share. If there is widespread agreement that the stock's price will grow significantly before the option expires, you may purchase a call option with a strike price of $100 per share. Assume for the purpose of argument that the choice costs $1. Because option pricing is given per share, you must pay $100 to purchase the option.

Assume that, before the option expires, the share price rises as projected, reaching $103 per share. You now have two options.

When the underlying stock's price rises, so does the value of the option contract. Perhaps the option price has raised to $1.50 per share. In such a situation, just sell the option and pocket the $0.50 per share profit.

You may also decide to use the option. This implies that you may purchase the shares at the strike price of $100 per share, even if the market price has climbed to $103 per share. So, because you spent $1 to acquire the option, your total cost is now $101 per share (assuming no fees, which is acceptable these days). So, you may now sell the stock on the open market for $103 per share, generating a profit of $2 per share. In other situations, investors may elect to retain the stock that they may now buy at a lower price.

Price of Breakeven

The breakeven price is an essential concept in options trading. The breakeven price for a call option is the strike price plus the amount paid per share to purchase the option. So, if you purchase a $212 strike price option for $2.50, the breakeven price is simply $212 + $2.50 = $214.50. This implies that the share price must climb to at least $214.50 before exercising the option is even worth considering; otherwise, as a buyer, you would lose money. The breakeven price is also critical for option sellers to consider. If you sell to open call options, you don't have to be concerned if the stock's market price remains at or below the breakeven point. In this case, a call option seller would be good if the stock price remained at or below $214.50.

The Seller of Calls

When a seller "writes" an option contract, it enters the market. Retail traders (individuals and small businesses) sell to open from a list of accessible alternatives. So, you'd locate a call option with a favorable expiry date and strike price, and then sell it using your brokerage software. There are three methods to sell a call option, the most basic of which is a covered call. This would need 100 shares of the underlying stock. Keep in mind that there is a possibility that you may lose ownership of the shares if the option is exercised and the shares are "called away" from you. However, a correctly chosen strike price and expiry date might reduce your risk. The purpose of selling a covered call option is to earn revenue from stock that you already own. Keep in mind that the breakeven price is something to keep an eye on in this scenario.

Call options may also be sold as part of one of the options strategies we'll look at later, such as an iron condor or a debit spread. In such methods, there is a single transaction involving several options that are purchased and sold, therefore you will never sell a single option utilizing a strategy.

Finally, you may sell a call option "naked," which implies you don't own any stock. To sell naked options, you must be a level four trader.

The call seller is in danger of being assigned. That is, if the share price climbs over the breakeven point, an option buyer may choose to execute the option. You will be allocated as a seller, which means you will be obliged to sell 100 shares of stock at the strike price. Many option articles claim that most options expire worthless, but the fact is that if the option you sold gets "in the money," there is a genuine possibility that the option will be exercised. In reality, options that expire in the money are often exercised automatically by the broker. Check with your broker to learn more about their rules.

Profitable Call Options

If you purchase call options, you are expecting to earn from either exercising the option or selling it at a profit. Because most beginner options traders will be dealing with modest amounts of cash, you are unlikely to be interested in executing the option. Rather, gains will be generated by the option itself. The value of a call option rises in tandem with the price of the underlying stock.

Because there are various elements at work in options pricing, you must consider more than simply the underlying price of the stock.

The expiry date is the most essential of them. Simply said, the longer an option is available before it expires, the more valuable it is.

The value in the option price is known as the time value, and it also contributes to the option's "extrinsic" value. The option's time value decreases with each passing day. You may really check the amount of value that an option will lose the next day, as we shall see next. That amount is immediately removed from the options price at market opening. That doesn't imply you can't keep options overnight, since other variables will be at work to raise the price of the option as well, and this may outweigh the price fall caused by the loss of time value. The term "time decay" refers to the loss of temporal value.

Out-of-the-money options are the most vulnerable to time decay, and if they are out of the money as the expiry date approaches, they might be worth almost nothing. When the option truly expires, it is worthless. That is why they "expire worthless".

The underlying share price on the open market is therefore the most crucial component in the option's pricing. In the case of a call option, the option's value rises whenever the share price rises. This is particularly noticeable for in-the-money options, but all call options will increase in value as the share price rises. So, on a day when the stock price rises significantly, you may make huge gains from out-of-the-money options. These swings do not have to be especially substantial; a single dollar gain in share price may result in a $50 to $100 increase in the option price. So, you may purchase an option in the morning and sell it for a $50 to $100 profit if the share price climbs by a dollar throughout the day. Profitability increases when the share price rises. While out-of-the-money options often offer lesser profit amounts for a given share price change, the rewards may still be significant.

So, for basic options trading, the concept of purchasing a call option is straightforward. You expect to purchase cheap and sell high, profiting from the underlying stock's upward price rise. The idea is to sell the option before it expires and before time decay consumes part or all of the profits (in the case of out-of-the-money options).

CHAPTER 7

PURCHASING AND SELLING PUTS

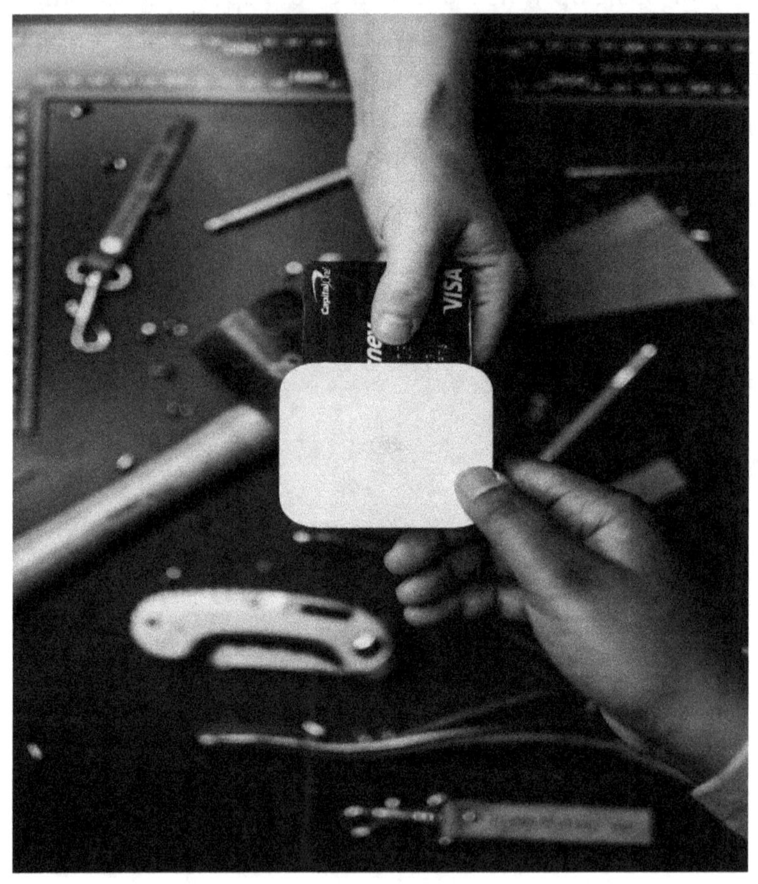

Option to Put

If you believe the price of a stock will fall, you may benefit by purchasing put options. Put options, like call options, may be used in a variety of ways. They have an expiry date, 100 shares of the underlying stock, and their price is determined by the underlying stock's price. Meanwhile, as the option's expiry date approaches, they suffer from time decay. Put options, on the other hand, gain value when the stock price falls and lose value when the stock price increases.

Put options may therefore be used to "short" the stock.

Shorting a stock is simply a term for profiting when the stock price falls. Shorting a stock usually works like this. If you believe a stock's value will fall, you borrow shares from your broker and promptly sell them on the market at the current stock price. Then, presuming your prediction was accurate, you purchase the shares back when the price falls. Assume, for the purpose of illustration, that you borrowed the shares and sold them for $100 a share. The price then falls to $80 per share, maybe due to a poor earnings call. When the price falls, you repurchase the shares for $80 per share and return them to the broker (remember, you began the process by borrowing shares from the broker). This exercise results in a profit of $20 per share.

Of course, most small investors don't have $10,000 or more to risk on scams like this, but put options allow you to benefit if a stock's price falls while making much smaller amounts. The concept is similar, but if you believe the price of a stock will fall in the near future, you may purchase put options on the stock. A put option, like a call option, has a strike price, and when the share price falls below the strike price, the put option is in the money. This is due to the fact that you would be able to purchase shares of stock at the market price and then sell them at the strike price, generating a profit in the process.

Using the same example as previously, you might purchase a put option with a strike price of $100. When the price of the shares fell to $80, you could acquire them on the open market and sell them to the creator of the put option contract at the strike price of $100 per share. Purchasing a put option does not need a huge margin account.

When a put option is executed, which means you sell the stock at the strike price, the stock is said to have been "put to" the option contract's originator. Of fact, most options traders aren't interested in exercising individual put options. If the stock price of a stock where you acquired put options with a $100 strike price dropped by $20 per share, the value of the put options would rise significantly since you might exercise them and profit handsomely. Because there are other traders interested in selling the stock, you will be able to profitably sell your put option to another trader. Remember that if you purchase to open an options contract, you are not tied to anything and may sell it to someone else at any time.

Consider putting options in the same manner as call options are, but with the price increasing by $100 every time the stock falls by $1. Put option price, like call option pricing, is influenced by a variety of circumstances, therefore this is an excellent connection to consider. However, it provides a rule of thumb for understanding how to put options function (the more money they are, the closer they are to the ideal scenario). Similarly, if the stock price increases by $1, the value of a put option falls by $100. So, it's an inverse connection with put options.

Why Should You Purchase Put Options?

When you purchase put options, you anticipate the value of a stock will fall. If a company's earnings call is disappointing, it may be a good opportunity to purchase a put option. Typically, the stock price may decline significantly, potentially over a day or two, before stabilizing at a new, lower level. Any form of unfavorable news gives a chance to benefit from put options. Being able to generate money while equities are decreasing is a kind of flexibility that most stock traders and investors do not have. The ability to open your eyes to the possibility of options in extending your capacity to benefit from the stock market. An options trader may earn from any potential scenario of stock market movement.

CHAPTER 8

NEW TRADER STRATEGIES LONG-TERM VS. SHORT-TERM STRATEGY

The adoption of a short-term plan is meant to generate as much money as possible in the short run, which means on a daily or weekly basis. In general, "short term" refers to something lasting less than a month. Naturally, some investors plan their actions on an hourly basis. As a result, the idea of "short-term" has varied degrees. It should be mentioned that short-term techniques are popular among new investors since they may limit risk by entering and leaving deals before major market movements occur.

As investors acquire expertise, they may develop a better understanding of how markets act, enabling them to remain in the game for a longer period of time.

The 20-Day System

This is one of the ways we employ to generate some quick money.

If you look at a recently rising stock, odds are it will fall precipitously over the next 20 days. This is true 99% of the time, which is why we prefer to wait 20 days before investing in a company. If you wait 20 days, you will reach the stock's lowest price point. It is best to invest in that stock while it is at its lowest point. The stock is likely to rise again; many top traders have used this strategy with great success. The secret is to wait at least 20 days before making a deal. Depending on the firm, stock prices will fall within 20 days following a significant increase. And on the 20th day, you put your money in that stock and watch it increase. Capital gains may be seen within 10 days after spending the money.

To carry out this technique, it's a good idea to get quite acquainted with the 10-day moving average of the stock or asset you want to buy. The 20-day strategy is comprised of two 10-day moving average phases. You can see where the stock's trend is by looking at this metric. This allows you to forecast where prices may climb or decrease. However, it is important to remember that deals lasting more than a week should not be considered. This is because 5 days is precisely half of the 10-day moving average. As a result, you may come in and out well before markets rebalance at the end of the week and again at the beginning of the week. It's usually a good idea to arrive early in the week and leave by Friday afternoon.

Don't sell until the stock price reaches a certain level. It has returned to its all-time high.

After you grasp the foundations of the 20-day technique, you should realize that you should not sell your stock until it has returned to its greatest stock price in those 20 days. When a company reaches its all-time low, it usually rises back up to its all-time high, if not higher, which is why it is recommended that you wait for the stock to grow back up to its highest point or higher. That is, you should not sell your stock until it has recovered to its maximum price point. A good rule of thumb is to wait another 20 days after investing your money. Except for the stock to soar back up to a price where it was at its maximum or even higher than that, you can surely withdraw that money and enjoy it after you've done that. We realize that you are always quite emotional when it comes to the money you invest.

A helpful piece of advice for first-time investors is to avoid being emotionally tied to a stock or a certain transaction. This is why options might assist you in removing the emotional component from trading.

The reason for this is that investors believe that if they hang on just a little longer, they will be able to balance their losses and regain some profit. This is a poor plan. As a result, it's always a smart idea to cut your losses and move on whenever possible.

Examine the Trend

When you are attempting to get short-term cash, you must begin to look at the pattern. Always keep an eye on current trends and invest your money properly. If you believe that a certain stock will rise in value quickly, make an investment in that stock. If you look at the transcript history, you should be able to tell which stocks will rise shortly and which will not. This will help you to achieve enormous monetary gains via options trading. When following trends, though, you must keep a watch on your stock. As far as trends go, they will rise swiftly and fall even faster. This is why it is recommended that they keep an eye on your stock as much as possible and pull the trigger when you believe it is appropriate. As usual, do not get emotionally tied to your investments, and if you believe they are gradually declining, consider selling them.

Reduce Risk

When it comes to trading, risk is an inherent component. As a result, it is critical that you manage risk in such a way that you can protect yourself if and when markets abruptly change. While this is not often, there is always the risk of an unexpected incident that causes investors to sell out immediately. In addition to buying options to hedge your assets, never invest more than 2% of your total investing money in a single deal. This distributes the risk among the different transactions you have going on at any one moment. So, if one sale goes bad, the most you may conceivably lose is 2%. On the contrary, if you invested, say, 50% of your money in one transaction and that transaction failed, you would lose half of your investment capital. Needless to say, this would be disastrous for your portfolio.

Stocks to Watch for Big Moves Coming Soon

This is one of the long-term/short-term strategy alternatives, similar to Trends. The method may be applied in both the long and short term. However, it is appropriate to engage in short-term options trading, and you should concentrate on equities that have a history of making substantial changes in a short period of time.

Long-Term Planning

We will discuss technical analysis and explain what it entails, as well as fundamental analysis. And then we'll assist you understand which strategy works best for what; once you grasp this, you'll be in a lot better position to make more money with options trading.

Technical Evaluation

To put it simply, technical analysis is a method through which Option Traders discover a framework for studying price movement. The basic idea behind this strategy is that a person would examine prior prices and changes to identify the present trading circumstances and prospective price movement. The main difficulty with this strategy is that it is philosophical, which means that every technical analysis is mirrored in price. The price represents the information that is available, and the price action is all that is required to make a transaction.

The technical analysis is based on history and trends, and traders will keep an eye on the past as well as the future, and based on that, they will determine whether or not to trade. More significantly, those who will trade using technical analysis will utilize history to assess whether they will make the deal or not. To test technical analysis, search up the trading price of a certain stock in the last five years. Many Option Traders utilized this to assess the past and future of the capital, as well as whether or not to trade using technical analysis. There are several charts available online that may help you understand how technical analysis works. However, we have included a quick description of the technical analysis.

Fundamental Examination

In the long run, fundamental analysis is more practical and achievable.

The whole idea of theoretical analysis is that you look at the country's economy and the trading system in place to evaluate if it is a smart trade or not. Because it focuses on economics, it may help you determine whether the dollar is rising or falling and what is driving it.

Understanding why a dollar is falling or rising is one of the most important things you can do when trading options. Once you grasp it, you will be in a lot better position to earn from your Option Trading attempts. Before deciding whether to use fundamental analysis, you will look at the country's employment and unemployment rate, as well as how training with various nations generally impacts the country's economy. Many effective option traders rely purely on fundamental research since it is factual, as opposed to technical analysis. Technical analysis, although correct, is not guaranteed in the same way that theoretical analysis is. Instead of focusing on trends, you will investigate what causes the highs and lows.

Not only that, but you will be able to predict the country's present and future economic picture based on the highs and lows. One rule of thumb to consider is how well the state is doing; the better the state is performing; the more foreign investors will participate in it. Once the piece is started, the dollar or stock in that nation will skyrocket.

The premise behind the basic analysis is that you must look at the country's economic situation as well as its political situation. To clarify, fundamental analysis is typically used when investing in a nation that is doing well in the economy, rather than investing in a firm that is performing poorly in the market. This makes sense given that the economy determines how much low prices will cost per dollar. Most investors will invest their money as soon as they see the value of the dollar rise. They will do so because they believe the dollar will continue to rise in value as the economy improves. One of the best instances would be when the US currency fell in 2007 and 2008, and the Canadian dollar rose in value; at that time, many investors were investing in Canadian dollars rather than US dollars.

After a lengthy period of decline, the US dollar fell precipitously, while the Canadian dollar was more costly than the US dollar. This was one of the oddities that occurred back then.

CHAPTER 9

HORIZONTAL SPREADS

Horizontal spreads, like vertical spreads, are two-leg transactions. They are simple to put up but might be difficult to examine prior to admission. This is because most horizontal spreads involve a time component that some people find confusing. Overall, the horizontal spread technique is one that is dependent on a little amount of chance.

However, when you do it properly, it makes it all worthwhile since the benefits are bigger when done correctly.

Spreadsheet for Call Calendars

Because of the way, the two legs of the trade are put up, horizontal spread trades are also known as calendar spreads. The call calendar spread is most effective after the early phase of a rally when the trend starts to decelerate. The nice thing about the calendar layout is that you can configure it to almost any time range you choose.

The first step is to open a long call position with an expiration date of at least 60 days after the trading date. The second leg is a short call position that expires in at least 30 days. The important thing to remember is that the long call should end after the short call. Both calls have the same strike price.

You can see where the terms horizontal and calendar originated.

Vertical spreads required you to trade calls and options with the same expiry month but different strike prices. We're looking at the same strike price but various expiry dates here.

This spreads the trade horizontally.

You may set the expiry date for the lengthy call to be more than 60 days or even 90 days away. Similarly, you may decrease the time frame for the short call, but keep in mind that if you move within the 30-day timeframe, time decay means you'll earn a lower premium when you write the option.

Should you extend the duration of the short call? You can, but as you'll see today, it's a hazardous move.

Commercial Property

A horizontal call spread allows you to have your cake and eat it as well. Uptrends might be glacial at times. They may be lengthy and drawn out, as well as travel sideways for extended periods of time without losing strength. Such behavior renders a short-term vertical spread unprofitable.

Consider opening a bull call spread expecting that the price will trend higher for a long period but then just sit there. While this is going on, your vertical spread trade is doing nothing and you are losing money. You could start a bull put spread, but this seems to be the worst thing to do.

What I mean is that if you know the trend will persist for a long period, why would you restrict your profit right away? It doesn't make any sense. This is when a horizontal trade makes considerably more sense since you can profit from both the short-term sluggishness and the long-term potential.

In technical words, such an opportunity will be seen in a trend where counter-trend presence has increased and ranges are persisting for a few weeks at a time. In such cases, the short call (with a closer expiration date) will assist you to catch the premium since the price is unlikely to reach it. When the price breaks out of the range and continues higher, the long call will move into the money, allowing you to benefit from the bull move. When it comes to horizontal trades, determining the right strike price is even more critical than in vertical spreads. Fortunately, it's not as complicated as it seems. You must consider the future resistance levels and choose a price above them. Take caution not to choose a level that is way too powerful.

Ideally, you want a level that is medium in strength and will last at least a month. Let's use TSLA as an example (market price $478.15) and use $500 as our optimum strike price. The 500-call will cost us $28.50 when it expires a month later. The 500-call expiring in 31 days will earn us a premium of $20, resulting in a net negative transaction of $8.50. The ideal case would be for TSLA to remain below 500 for a month or more before rising over it, ensuring that both legs perform adequately.

If the deal does not go as planned, you may switch to a different approach. Assume TSLA is poised to break through 500 in the next month. You may now change the transaction to a bull call spread. You may close your short call position and establish a new one that expires in the same month as the long call.

Similarly, if TSLA falls significantly and is unlikely to break through 500 anytime soon, you may change the trade to a bear call spread.

It all depends on how you interpret the current market situation.

Spreads on Puts

You may profit from putting spreads in the same way that you can from call spreads. Again, none of the following methods involve underlying stock ownership, therefore the risk and margin necessary to build a position are considerably decreased.

In some circumstances, a number of these spread transactions may be turned into collars. Keep this in mind as we go since it is not always practical to mention every single exit circumstance.

Remember the prerequisites for a good collar trade and, after reading the techniques, attempt to identify how you might transform them into lucrative collars.

These tactics will earn you money in bullish, bearish, and neutral market conditions.

Chapter 10:

STRADDLES AND STRANGLES

To complete our look at options trading methods, we'll look at straddles and strangles. Combination trades are what they're called. This is because they require beginning legs that include both calls and puts. These transactions are a step up in terms of complexity, but as long as you grasp the theory behind them, you'll find that monitoring them isn't too tough. So, first, let's look at straddles.

Straddles

Unlike spread trades, which have a directional bias, combination trade methods are unconcerned about the market's movement. In these methods, volatility is key.

As a result, any explanation of these methods will include a sprinkling of so-called 'Greeks,' which are volatility measurements, as well as other complex ideas.

However, even if you aren't the world's finest specialist in straddles (or strangles), you can do them quite well. The straddle's principle is straightforward. You aren't concerned with the market's direction as much as you are with the degree to which it will move.

All of the tactics we've looked at thus far have included technical analysis components. To put it another way, none of them have been essentially basic in character. Combination trades may be carried out utilizing just fundamental variables. Special events, macroeconomic releases, earnings announcements, lawsuit announcements, and other factors might be utilized to screen for straddle chances. Let us now examine the trade's structure.

Structure of Trade

The transaction has two legs. The first is a close-to-the-money long put, while the second is a close-to-the-money long call. Because both legs are lengthy, you don't need to care about the sequence in which you insert the trading legs. It is critical to ensure that the expiry dates of both legs are the same.

This is the perfect circumstance. The underlying erupts in either direction in a flash of volatility. You are in an excellent position to gain regardless of what occurs if you have long options that capture both sides of the market. The notion is that the magnitude of price movement will be sufficient to offset any premium paid to join the opposite side of the trade.

This generates a zone around the present market price that serves as a profit barrier for the price. You will not earn any money as long as the price stays within these limits. As a result, there are two things that are critical when it comes to straddles.

The first step is to decide how far apart you want your long option legs to be.

The second step is to see whether the expected volatility of the underlying is correct. This may be accomplished by examining the underlying's implied volatility. Expect major movements as long as it remains over its historical limitations.

How close to the market price should your option strike prices be?

In this case, there is a tradeoff between volatility and the distance between the strike price and the market price. The lower the volatility you anticipate, the closer your strike prices must be. However, the closer you get to the position, the greater the premium you will have to pay to enter it.

The larger the premium, the higher the price barrier that must be crossed in order for you to profit. As a result, being as near to market pricing as feasible isn't necessarily a desirable thing. Let's have a look at how this works using TSLA as an example.

How Does It Work?

The current market price of TSLA is $478.15. Assume that earnings season has arrived and experts are divided on TSLA's prospects. Some predict that if TSLA fails to meet expectations, the business would lose even more market share to its conventional auto sector competitors. They also believe that if TSLA demonstrates substantial profit growth, it would be a good signal that the firm is on track.

As you can imagine from such a situation, the price of TSLA will either rise drastically or fall dramatically. While directional traders are busy determining which way the stock is likely to go, you may take the simple route and just use a straddle.

Assume you choose a $525 long call strike price and a $430 long put strike price. Entering the call leg will cost you $15.35 while entering the put leg will cost you $11.80. As a result, your trade entrance fee is $27.15. This is also the barrier that TSLA's price must clear in order to turn a profit.

Recognize that there are two obstacles here. The first barrier is created by strike pricing. Before you can even think about gains, the stock price must climb or fall to at least the level of the strike prices. The premium must then rise by at least $27.15 before you may benefit financially. In this situation, the increase in intrinsic value should guarantee that the option premium crosses the financial barrier if either option becomes profitable.

In terms of expiration dates, you may choose either the current month or the month following. Given that the options set to expire the next month will have a full-time value, you can expect to pay a higher premium for them. As a result, it is preferable to take advantage of time decay and purchase choices for the current month.

Strangles

Now that you understand how straddles operate, let's take a quick look at strangles. I say short because strangles and straddles are the same approach. It's only that the option strike prices are spread out wider in expectation of even more volatility than with the straddle.

Both trades have the same number of legs and use the same techniques to put them up. As long as you understand one, executing the other shouldn't be too difficult.

CHAPTER 11:

MONEY AND RISK MANAGEMENT

Markets Rhythmic and Cyclical Alph Nelson Elliott devised a method for interpreting wave market movements. His study, which focuses on hourly Dow Jones quotes and was published in 1938, sparked attention owing to the creation of fractals and chaotic movements.

This study takes into account an alternating of unexpected and deterministic periods. As Burton Malkiel suggested, markets would not be controlled by a random walk. Mandelbrot elaborates on this point in his book Fractals, Chance, and Finance. He believes that the development of prices is discontinuous, that prices might move abruptly rather than gradually and continuously, as good and poor weather do: "If the markets were perfect, they would react to all news instantly," he remarked. They now take their time integrating information and occasionally exaggerate their efforts.

Elliott's study led him to the following conclusion: the stock market's constant fluctuations reflect a basic harmony of nature. Thus, he observes that changes in the Dow Jones Industrial Average (DJIA) create observable figures that return in the same patterns, but with varying length and magnitude.

These discoveries will enable him to establish Elliott's Wave Theory. It blends the psychological component introduced by Charles Dow with the natural harmony established by the mathematician Fibonacci. It is made up of a collection of empirical criteria that are used to understand the development of major stock indexes. This technique is effective because Elliott's rules and principles are intended to include all market activity. The fundamental benefit of the Elliott Wave Method is that it allows you to create scenarios, establish objectives, and have points of invalidation while also knowing the universe of possibilities.

This method is appealing because it enables one to evaluate the cyclicality of financial markets. Indeed, stock prices advance in a cyclical fashion: a gain or a fall will never occur in time and will be interrupted by consolidation or corrective movements. Elliott was one of the first authors to emphasize the notion of action/reaction, which states that each impulsive movement must be followed by a corrective movement, with the impulsive movement having a greater amplitude than the corrective movement.

In an uptrend, for example, the amplitude of impulsive (bullish) waves is often greater than that of corrective (down) waves, and vice versa.

It is evident that the market might explode following an impetuous movement during a notable trend. Profit-taking is a simple explanation for this phenomenon. New entrants (buyers in an uptrend and sellers in a downtrend) are waiting for the existence of a low point to position themselves, allowing the dominating trend to resume. The major strength of Elliott's waves is that it is a comprehensive strategy that stresses the two most crucial components in trading: price and time.

Elliott Wave Analysis

Elliott said in different articles published in the Financial World in 1939 that the market's bottom rate was a cycle of eight waves, including five waves of increase and three waves of drop.

The three waves of decline constitute a corrective to the prior five waves of growth.

Elliott believes that every impulsive activity is followed by a corrective response. An impulsive movement is made up of five lower-degree waves, three of which are impulsive and two of which are corrective.

The corrective movement is made up of three waves: two corrective and one impulsive.

We shall begin by describing the five waves that comprise the impulsive movement:

The first wave indicates the commercial entry of predecessors.

The latter predicts a market reversal and the impending impulsive movement. They want to go back to the inception of the movement, to the initiated investors indicated by Charles Dow.

The second wave is often a powerful corrective to the initial impulsive movement. It shows the entrance of contrarians who are betting on the drop because they feel the market is still in a negative period.

Typically, the third wave consists of followers and professional investors.

The news is good, and the operators are hurrying to get their hands on the title, generating a rapid upward acceleration. The strong impulsive wave is seldom the shortest.

Profit-taking by operators who took advantage of a wave's strong climb is the fourth wave. Nonetheless, the trend remains optimistic and is unassailable.

The fifth wave is the last impulsive wave of significant impulsive movement. It refers to the admission of late followers, who have seen the ascent without situating themselves and are ready to join others in enjoying the movement. In general, they are the first to suffer from a market slump. This wave is also distinguished by the depletion of technical indicators, which often show a bearish divergence and indicate the exhaustion of the trend in progress as well as the imminence of a correction.

It is fairly commonplace to see an "extension" on many impulsive waves: this is a wave of impulse that is extended and shows the strength of the wave in question. This extension generally takes the form of a single impulsive wave, allowing analysts to measure additional waves. As a result, if the first and third waves have the same duration, the fifth will almost surely be an extension. Elliott's criteria are intended to capture all of the market's activity.

This breakdown, according to Elliott, can be discovered regardless of the time selected. Some analysts are quick to draw parallels with the chaos theory produced, in particular, by Mandelbrot. This idea proposes that there is order in seeming chaos and that photographs collected at various scales (short term, long term) may have surprising parallels. They overlook, however, that Mandelbrot, the primary involved, does not take Elliott's waves seriously. But set aside these frivolous debates and consider the most significant point: this strategy is popular, it is followed (the trader must, therefore, include it in his armory), and it is even occasionally successful!

Four fundamental principles and five rules

Elliott's waves are governed by various concepts, which we shall simplify into core principles:

Markets never rise all at once; impulse waves, movements in the direction of the primary tendency, are decomposed into five waves of a lower degree, and corrective waves, movements against the primary trend (bullish or bearish), are decomposed into three waves of a lower degree.

When an eight-wave movement (five up and three down) finishes, a full cycle ends and this cycle becomes two subdivisions in the immediately higher degree wave; regardless of time horizon, the method of counting is the same since the market is moving at the same rate. The specified guidelines must be strictly followed throughout a count and will be monitored over time.

Correctional Waves

Corrective waves come in a variety of shapes (zigzags, flats, etc.). Corrective waves always correct the preceding upward movement in a 5-step movement. The following are the most often observed properties: wave 2 corrects Wave 1, and Wave 4 corrects Wave 3.

Elliott and many other top-tier analysts discovered that corrective waves frequently corrected a portion of impulsive moves.

Typical Wave Retracement Ratios 2

Wave 2 is often the strongest and corrects waves 1 and 3. It tracks the previous move at a minimum of 38.2% to 50%, but the average retracement is 61.8% and may reach 76.4%.

Retracement Ratios for Standard Waves 4

Profit-taking is represented by Wave 4. The correction is seldom severe and always stands at least at 23.6%, the norm is 38.2%, and they never retrace more than 50%. If the correction is larger than 50%, its count should be questioned since it is most likely wave 1.

In summary, Wave 2 corrects substantially (61.8% is the typical ratio), but Wave 4 profits (38.2% is the standard ratio).

Can We Tell the Difference Between a Corrective Wave and a True Trend Reversal?

We've seen before how an upswing might be called into doubt when a lower precedent is depressed. A correction was then drawn, and prices fell below the two prior low marks without stopping the title from continuing to rise.

This corrective movement, in fact, corrects the whole prior movement.

If and only if the corrective wave lowers the low point of the prior impulsive movement, the corrective movement corresponds to a real trend reversal. If not, the existing trend will continue and nothing will call it into doubt.

The Alternation Rule

This rule is a strong Elliott's wave concept. The premise is simple: if wave 2 corrects heavily, wave 4 will correct less strongly. If wave 2 corrects weakly, anticipate an impulsive wave 3 as well as a strong corrective in wave 4.

The second attribute of alternation rules is dependent on the correction's simplicity or complexity. A simple wave 2 is generally followed by a complicated wave 4. In contrast, if Wave 2 is complicated, Wave 4 will be simple.

Waves that are impulsive in nature

Fibonacci ratios bind impulsive waves together. Thus, the aim of wave 3 is often reached by multiplying the length of wave 1 by 1.618 and deferring the result obtained at the bottom of wave 2. Wave 3 will often get to this aim before correcting in wave 4. However, with forceful extension motions, the ratio will be more than 1,618. The following ratios are often used: 2-2,618-3, and so on.

If wave 2 is only partially traced (less than 50%), anticipate a strong wave 3 with ratios above the norm of 1.618.

Advantages

The major benefit of Elliott's wave approach is that it encourages the analyst and trader to envisage alternative counts, which is good training for dealing with many scenarios.

A competent "Elliottist" is never satisfied, and he will always emphasize a preferred scenario (the one with the highest possibility of unfolding) and an alternative (a situation that would invalidate his ideal scenario) in his analysis.

Disadvantages

The first drawback of Elliott waves is the amount of time it takes to study them. Is it necessary to justify the time spent on training Elliott's waves?

I would respond that although it is interesting for a trader to understand the principles of Elliott's waves, the indications generated by this strategy do not seem to be persuasive enough to invest too much effort.

Many stakeholders are captivated by Elliott's waves to the point of slavery. This approach allows for the identification of turning points with dizzying accuracy. However, the pitfall of this kind of analysis is that it forces the countdown in a circumstance where none seems to exist. The analyst then persists in looking for movement on five occasions when none exists.

This hazard is vividly shown by the well-known Elliott Wave Advisor Prechter, who became renowned in 1987 for using this approach to anticipate the stock market collapse. In the 1990s, his market forecast was exceedingly pessimistic, and he repeatedly warned the media that the US market was poised to enter a lengthy bear market. This analyst was suffocated by his approach. He fell in love with it rather than seeing it for what it is: a straightforward analytical instrument.

The conclusion of this tale is twofold: markets are always correct, and traders who reject this truth may pay dearly.

CHAPTER 12:

EVALUATING MARKET MOOD SWINGS'

Modern markets are so unpredictable that a straightforward buy-and-hold strategy, even over the long term, is no longer viable.

The market is rising.

A bullish market is distinguished by a series of lower and higher points, as well as higher and higher points. In a definite uptrend, the corrective phases (down legs) have a lower amplitude than the impulsive phases (raising legs). This feature is very significant since it indicates the likelihood of a trend reversal. When the amplitude of a corrective leg exceeds that of an impulsive leg (bullish in a bull market), the uptrend is likely to be challenged. The trader must reassess the present trend and avoid setting himself up for a buy under these circumstances.

A downtrend market has lower and higher points, as well as lower and lower points. Rebounds in this market frequently have less amplitude than bearish legs, which is the key feature of a bear market. In a trending market, moves in the direction of the main trend continue to be the most powerful. In terms of the upswing, a turnaround is possible. This necessitates a greater comeback than the last bearish wave.

The Trendless Market

There is no discernible trend in a trendless market, and low and high points are often mistaken. Buyers and sellers are putting themselves to the test, and there is no apparent consensus at work.

According to Wilder, markets develop in trend one-third of the time and do not show any apparent pattern the other two-thirds of the time. This attribute is significant because investors are often victims of momentum bias. They have a tendency to mechanically extend the most recent course progression. If the path continues to increase in the previous few sessions, they are persuaded that it will continue to rise, and many traders are caught by setting themselves around resistance or slightly above 2. In the event of a stock price decrease, investors believe that the downturn will continue and are stuck by establishing a position around critical support.

A competent trader can patiently wait for the proper opportunity to initiate a position. Professional traders attempt to position themselves before the start of an impulsive movement in order to prevent exposure by taking needless risks while the market is unpredictable. People who can adjust to shifting market circumstances become good traders. Markets vary differently depending on whether we are in an upswing, a negative trend, or a trending market, as we shall see later. In a bullish (bearish) market, the trader may afford to purchase (sell) higher (lower) and sell (buy) even higher (lower), even if it is not optimal.

The Trend Lines

Traders often use trend lines to pinpoint bullish peaks in an uptrend and highs in a downturn. The trend line in a bull market passes through at least two low points. In a down-trending market, the trend line will connect at least two high points. Trends may be adjusted over time depending on new information: sharper, more distinct trends may arise when the trend first identified becomes outdated.

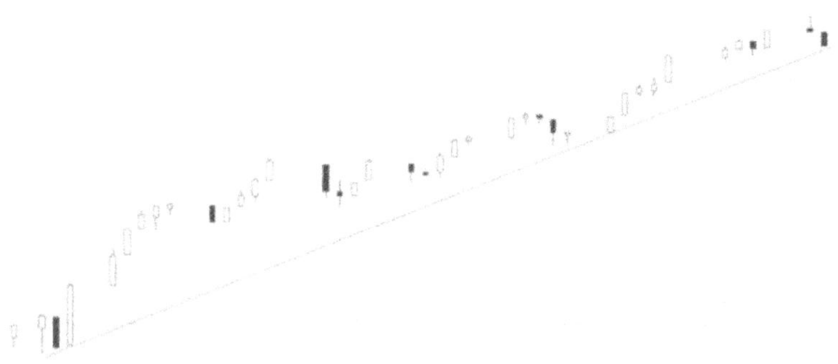

Trend Line Effectiveness Conditions

The efficiency of trend lines in finding good levels of support and resistance justifies their success. In other words, they may occasionally provide these tiny degrees of reversal with astonishing accuracy when a trend has already begun.

They also allow you to assess the status of the trend and anticipate reversals or simply corrective moves. In what follows, we will attempt to provide some aspects to explain their efficacy.

One method promotes the claim that stock market development is a "natural" process. Trends would exist on the market and overall time horizons that would adhere to a rate of advancement and hence a certain angle. According to the famed trader and analyst WD Gann, a trend line must have a 45-degree angle in order to endure. Not to mention natural phenomena, a sequence of courses with a low slope implies a sluggish movement that will most likely abort. When the slope is steep, the movement is overly impetuous and runs out of steam rapidly. The aim is to have an average slope (45 degrees), which indicates a healthy impulsive movement.

Another strong argument in favor of trend lines is that most traders are familiar with them. As we have seen, the phenomena of self-fulfilling prophesies will boost their validity. In practice, a bullish trader will construct a trend line to highlight the likely drop-off point for the stock, indicating a solid purchase with little risk. In the opposite instance, a downtrend line will be drawn to highlight sales levels.

The significance of a trend line is determined by the number of points it links. The bigger the number of rebounds on the right, the more significant the relevance. This is explained in particular by the mimicking of operators, which strengthens the line. Furthermore, trend lines may be plotted across a variety of time periods (long, medium, and short term), but long-term trend lines, or simply to take them, are the most reliable. The trader will benefit from a return to the right of support (resistance) to enhance its buying (selling) position, particularly as the trend's validity is proved.

Identifying a Trend Reversal Making Use of a Trend Line

The breaking of a trend line is a significant reversal indicator. This signal is much stronger since the trend line is substantial (it has been used to support the present trend on several occasions). The break of a bullish or bearish straight line signals the end of a market dynamic: the operators who should have strengthened their positions near the trend line proved to be weaker than the opposing side (the bears), allowing the right and all market dynamics to be ruptured. As a result, the shift in trend seems to be obvious.

A broken bullish straight line instantly becomes a line of resistance against which the market will collapse; this is often shown by a pullback (return to the right of a recently broken trend). As a result, the market assesses the strength of the support that has turned into resistance (or vice versa). Be cautious; a breach of a trend line cannot alone signify a market reversal, as shown by the example of the title PPR. It only informs the trader of the probability of consolidation.

Channels or Canals

A channel (Canal) is a figure that is closely connected to the preceding trend line analysis. The tracking is straightforward: once a bullish trend has been identified, it is only a matter of identifying a parallel to the propensity to cover the whole price development. We acquire a channel in which the courses develop harmoniously across the time when the trend is recorded (straight line linking the extreme points).

The channel will tuck into a trend by enabling impulsive turning points to be found via trend lines, but it will also enable corrective turning points to be determined through the top channel of an uptrend channel - or the bottom line of a downtrend channel.

The courses, therefore, fluctuate between these two lines: the first is the canal's support line, where the courts rest; the second is the channel's resistance line (or top of the channel), against which the market stumbles.

Trends may be divided into three categories: short-term, medium-term, and long-term. The significance of a channel is determined not only by its length of development but also by the number of times each line of the channel has been altered. A canal must have at least two effects on each side to be evaluated. The greater the number of effects, the more significant the channel.

Lines in the Middle

In actuality, prices do not move inexorably between the lower and higher bounds. They can have difficulty navigating through intermediate portions of the canal. Parallel straight lines to the channel may be drawn to represent as many lines of support or mild resistance for the courses. However, the number of genuine intermediate rights is limited; often, one or two are found. They are often midway through the channel and serve as true tests to see if the courses will reach the top or bottom. In the event of a bullish channel, a break in the intermediate resistance line often suggests that the market will reach the channel's top.

It is also feasible to discern minor intermediary channels inside a channel that enable the market to shift from one terminal to another. Occasionally, a new channel arises inside the canal that becomes more significant and will ultimately replace the previous one that has become outdated.

Canal rupturing

There are two types of breaks that can occur: either the trend is confirmed and reinforced (it is an upward outflow of an uptrend channel or a decline of a downtrend channel), or it is reversed, indicating a possible trend change (downward release of a bullish channel and exit up a downtrend channel). Because the break is done in great volume, it is much more powerful.

The operator has numerous factors to recognize a likely channel rupture: in the event of a downward departure of a bullish channel, we generally note that the courses have no strength, they do not come more to cross the intermediate right but stumble against it frequently. These are often the initial warning signs.

Precautions When a Signal Is Detected

Breaking a bullish channel does not always indicate a sell signal, and breaking a bearish channel does not always indicate a buy signal. This is a basic indicator that must be supplemented by additional parts in order to create a meaningful signal.

How Can You Tell When a Trend Is Over?

Can chart analysis be used to detect trend reversals? We shall see that it is feasible to trace a reversal visually, but the trader must ensure that three requirements are met: It is necessary to have a clear trend (for example, a trend line whose impulsive movements have a greater amplitude than corrective movements); the breaking of a major trend line or major support is often a precursor signal of reversal; and finally, various studies show that a large turnaround figure (which took some time to form) will frequently be at the origin of an important corrective movement.

The Reversal of Trend

Following a downward movement (bullish), the title depicts a bullish leg (bearish) with a bigger amplitude than the preceding bearish (bullish) leg. This arrangement implies a likely trend reversal and the imminence of a bullish (bearish) departure or simply the termination of the present trend and the entrance of the market into a phase without a trend.

This trend depiction has been purposefully simplified since the range of movements is considerably broader. However, before refining the study, it is critical to have a thorough understanding of the key market trends. The AGF stock is an example of a stock that has a robust rise with minimal corrections. A buyer couldn't identify a low point that would enable him to position himself in the direction of the trend.

How Do Trends Emerge?

Trends are a constant occurrence in markets, but their training is often misinterpreted by operators. Dow has established a hypothesis that may be applied to current markets, regardless of the time period employed, to give meaningful explanations for this phenomenon.

CHAPITRE 13:

BROKERS

When it comes to choosing brokers, you have numerous possibilities. There are full service, cheap, internet, and other options.

Understanding the distinctions between them and picking the finest ones for your needs is critical if you want to succeed. Another area that many newcomers disregard and subsequently pay the price for is the restrictions around options trading.

There aren't many regulations to follow, but they do have important implications for your capital and risk management techniques.

Selecting a Broker

In general, there are two types of brokers: discount brokers and full-service brokers. In reality, many full-service brokers already have discount operations, so there will be some overlap. A full-service business is one in which brokerage is just one component of a bigger financial supermarket.

Other investment options, estate planning techniques, and so on may be recommended by the broker. They'll also have an in-house research department that will provide you with studies to assist you trade more effectively. In addition, they will provide phone help if you have any queries or desire to make an order.

A full-service broker will become a fantastic company to network with if you have a solid connection with them. Every broker appreciates a lucrative client since it helps in marketing. A full-service broker will have solid industry ties and can put you in touch with the correct individuals if you have unique requirements.

The cost of all of this service is that you will pay more commissions than the norm. It is up to you to choose if this is a reasonable price to pay. As a result, in order to trade effectively, you do not need to join up with a full-service broker.

Order matching is done electronically these days, so it's unlikely that a person on the floor can get you a lower price. As a result, a full-service firm will not provide you with greater execution.

Discount brokers, on the other hand, are all about narrowing their focus. They just assist you in trading. They will not give guidance, at least not on purpose from a commercial standpoint, and phone ordering is non-existent. This does not imply a decrease in customer service. That is far from the case.

Commissions will be far cheaper than what you would expect to spend at a full-service brokerage.

A disadvantage of using a discount brokerage is that you will not obtain any specific product suggestions or solutions outside of your speculative activity. Many consumers choose to trade (through a separate account) with the same broker that manages their retirement assets, keeping everything in-house.

So, which one should you go with? So, if you want to keep your prices as low as possible, go with a discount broker. In fact, you should only use a full-service broker if you want to store everything in one location. Otherwise, there is no difference between the two alternatives these days.

Margin

The quantity of assets you now have in your account is referred to as your margin. Cash and positions are your assets. The amount of margin you have changed with the market value of your investments.

Margin is an essential topic to understand since it is central to your risk management practice.

You will have a choice when you establish an account with your broker. You have the option of opening a cash or margin account. To trade options, you must first create a margin account. To summarize, a cash account does not have leverage, thus you can only trade equities with it. There are no account minimums for a cash account, and if there are, they are rather small.

A margin account, on the other hand, is governed by entirely different regulations. For starters, margin account minimum balances are greater.

Most brokers have a $10,000 minimum deposit, and some may even raise it depending on your trading style. The account minimum accomplishes nothing on its own, but it serves as a type of commitment for the broker.

The assumption is that with this much money at stake, the trader will be more serious about it and will not blow it away. If only it were that simple. In any case, the minimum balance is an unbreakable norm. The Pattern Day Trader (PDT) label is another regulation to be mindful of.

PDT is a regulation issued directly by the SEC. A PDT is someone who executes four or more transactions within five days ("Pattern Day Trader," 2019). Once you've been assigned this tag, your broker will need you to deposit at least $25,000 in the margin as a minimum balance. Again, this minimal amount has no effect, but the SEC believes that if you do make a mistake, this will provide enough of a cushion.

Will the methods in this book qualify you as a PDT? This is all up to you. Each plan plays out over a month or more, so after you enter, all you have to do is watch it and, if necessary, alter it. However, if you want to avoid the PDT, you may only apply for three opportunities every workweek.

My recommendation is to research the tactics and begin gently. Start with one instrument and see how it goes, then expand as your confidence grows. You'll have gained enough experience by then to determine how much capital you'll need. Remember that even closing out a position is considered a trade, thus PDT does not just apply to trade entrance.

Call for Margin

Another component of margin that you should be aware of is the margin call.

Most traders, particularly institutional ones, fear this warning. The goal of all risk management is to keep you as far away from this occurring to you as possible. A margin call is issued when there is insufficient cash in your account to meet the account's needs.

Remember that your margin is the sum of your cash and the value of your holdings. If you have $1000 in cash but your position is now losing -$900, you will get a margin call to deposit additional cash to cover the possible loss. In fact, you'll get it ahead of schedule. If you do not post extra margin, your broker has the authority to close down your positions and collect whatever cash they can in order to prevent their risk limits from being activated.

The maintenance margin is the amount over which your broker will issue a margin call. Typically, you must keep 25% of your original position value (when you initiate a trade) in cash in your account. Most brokers include a helpful indication that shows how near you are to the limit.

Leverage is the most common source of margin calls. A margin account allows you to borrow money from your broker and utilize it to improve your profits. Consider the following scenario: if you trade with $10,000 of your own money and borrow $20,000 from your broker to take a position, you own $30,000 of the position. Assume this stake gains $10,000, bringing its total worth to $40,000.

You've just gotten a 100% return on this investment (since you only spent $10,000), despite the fact that the overall return on the position is 33% (10,000/30,000). But what happens if you lose $10,000 on the position? So, despite the position dropping just 33%, you just lost 100%. The use of leverage is a two-edged sword. It is much too basic to label leverage as either positive or harmful. That's all there is to it. Under no circumstances should you borrow money to trade if you are a newbie. When you're more experienced, you can do it as much as you want.

Please keep in mind that I'm distinguishing between leverage where you borrow money and the kind of leverage options give. With options, a single contract provides you power over a bigger portion of the stock, but the option premium must still be paid. As a result, trading options are less expensive than trading ordinary stock. If you borrow money to pay for the option premium, you are engaging in risky activity and should refrain. There is a distinction between having leverage built into the instrument and employing leverage to raise the quantity of anything you can purchase.

When you're a beginner, you should avoid the latter.

Execution

Complaining about execution is a favorite activity of failed traders. Their losses are always the fault of the broker, and if it weren't for the greedy brokers, they'd be rolling in it like Scrooge McDuck. Complaining about your execution will not help you. One of the main reasons for these concerns is that most new traders are unaware that the price they see on the screen is not the same as what is exchanged on the exchange.

We live in an age of high-frequency trading, and the smallest unit of time in the markets has shifted from seconds to microseconds. Trades are continually coming in, and the matching engine is always on the lookout for acceptable vendors for purchasers. Given the market's speed, it is critical to recognize that determining the precise price of an item is difficult.

As a result, in your risk management strategy, you must account for periods of high volatility, when the variations will be greater. For the time being, I want you to realize that just because the price you got differed from what was shown on the screen does not imply that the broker is inept.

How can you tell if a broker is incompetent? The best indications are customer service and the quality of the trading terminal to which you have access. Your broker is not out to defraud you or trade against you. This is not the case with FX, but we're not talking about FX in this book. So, instead of blaming your broker, look at your systems, providing the broker passes basic due diligence.

Price Estimates

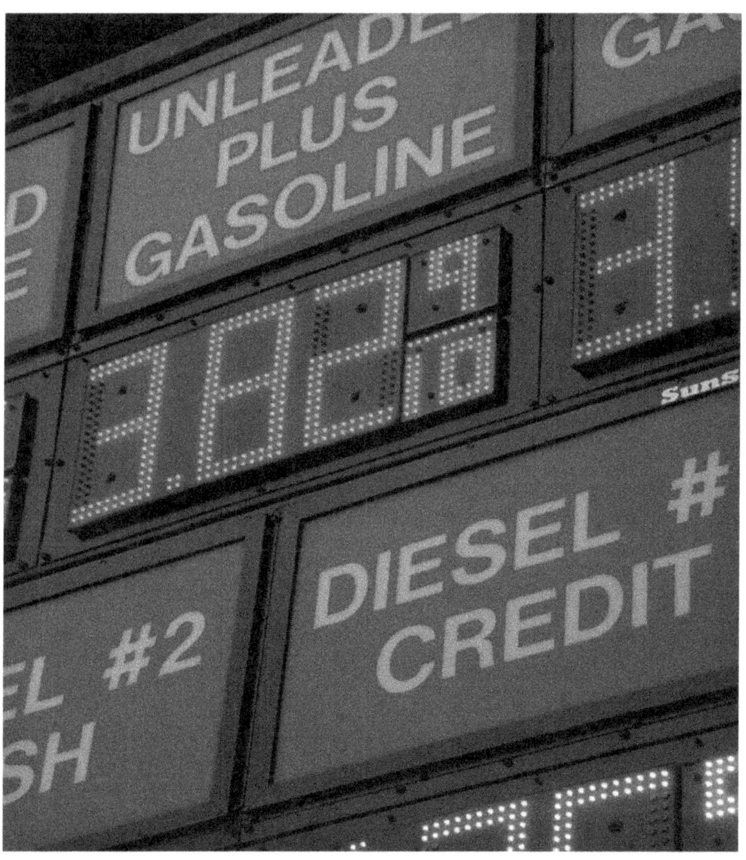

Many traders are perplexed when they first glance at their trading displays and see that everything has two prices. After all, every financial channel only shows one price for a security, but when you trade, you'll be given two separate prices inside the price box. This is a little yet critical point for you to grasp.

The lower price is known as the bid, and it is the amount you will pay if you sell the instrument. The greater the price, the higher the ask, and this is what you will spend to purchase the instrument. The single price shown on your TV screen is known as the "Last Traded Price," or LTP. Because the market is continuously moving, do not assume that the LTP is the true price.

Because of the continual fluctuation, even the spread (the gap between the ask and bid) does not adequately represent the genuine state of affairs. But there's no reason to be concerned; as long as volatility remains consistent, the difference isn't significant. Just remember to check the spread to see how much you'll be spending. The spread expands and contracts regularly, but if it becomes too large, it indicates that there is too much volatility and you should avoid trading.

This finishes our examination of brokers and their workings. As you can see, there isn't much to be worried about, but you should be informed since it affects how much cash you'll be dealing with. In general, the more cash you have, the safer you'll be since you'll have more space to make errors.

CHAPTER 14:

TECHNICAL ANALYSIS AND ITS FUNDAMENTALS

Whatever vehicle you choose for your activities, there are certain fundamentals that you must understand. This basic understanding is mostly related to market behavior. If you can understand how they act, you will be able to predict price movement more precisely, allowing you to make better trading selections. It is worth noting that regardless of the value exchanged on the market, some notions may always apply to prices and their performance on the market.

This may be explained by the fact that short-term price swings are caused by independent traders and investors. We may argue that the price is determined by the activities of those who invest or trade values on the market and that prices respond similarly when given comparable input or stimulus. Technical analysis is the study of price behavior, and knowing its fundamentals is one of the most important education points that you will need to be able to make accurate financial judgments on the market.

The Fundamentals of Technical Analysis

Technical analysis is a vast subject. If you decide to join the market and become an investor, you will almost certainly find yourself returning to study and learn something new regularly throughout the duration of your trading career. As a result, anybody skilled in options trading would suggest that a basic comprehension of technical analysis is a critical step for everyone active in the market. However, you do not need to know everything right now. Because it is a broad field of study, it is acceptable to limit your research to portions of the technical analysis that are especially relevant to that specific project. For example, technical analysis provides over a hundred indications for market analysis. In practice, traders often utilize three or four, mostly the most popular or those with which they are already acquainted. If you don't only trade options, but trade in general, you'll discover that technical analysis can be used for any financial asset, such as futures or stocks. Their foundation may be found in psychology and human nature in general, as well as how people behave in practice. We will go through some of the important issues in technical analysis to help you comprehend them better. These subjects will include the basis of technical analysis; how to chart principles and trends; patterns in technical analysis; technical analysis via the movement of averages; and indicators in technical analysis.

The cornerstone of technical analysis

The word "market activity" serves as the foundation for technical analysis. The market activity reflects your whole own understanding of the trading market and excludes information obtained from an insider. It is simply described as research that indicates "how the price changes over time". It also investigates its volumes and how they vary over time, if feasible.

Nonetheless, the core principle of technical analysis is founded on the assumption that market behavior is a reflection of all that has occurred and will happen with the price at a given time.

Many factors may influence the price, and the magnitude of the effect varies depending on the market in which the deal is done. That's where technical analysis comes in; it cuts through all of those possibilities and asserts that all we may know about the price is already contained in the price we see at the time we wish to trade.

This implies that you shouldn't worry too much about the factors that impact the price, since following how the price varies over time will provide you with all of your answers. Many individuals first questioned if this type of theory could work since it seemed so simple. If you had any questions, the answer has already been demonstrated, and it states that yes, technical analysis is effective, despite the fact that this kind of definition does not seem to be that complex.

However, one very crucial aspect emerges from all of this. Technical analysis cannot guarantee price behavior.

It can predict whether the price will rise or fall over a certain time period, although this is not always the case. It may or might not. The reason for this is that, regardless of the calculation that the market must act, it is hard to be certain that it will. The market has its own methods of doing things and finally gets what it wants.

So, what technical analysis does is give you an indicator of what the most likely conclusion will be, which means that the only certainty you have is whether the law of probability is on your side or not.

You may execute a lot of typical transactions and hopefully gain some money, but you should never invest money or precious commodities like your home or vehicle if you can't afford to lose them. It is not advised, particularly if one successful transaction has convinced you that only one is sufficient to be a solid technical signal for guaranteed gain. This is one of the reasons why the initial job of technical analysis is to increase your chances of success by evaluating pricing and market behavior.

The second rationale for the study is that prices virtually always move in response to specific patterns. For example, if the price rises, it will continue to climb until something prevents it from rising higher. Prices, in contrast, behave similarly to Newton's motion law, which states that "a body in motion will remain in motion until acted upon by an external force." Of course, for this to be shown, it must occur over time. If this were not the case, the price charts shown in numerous analyses would not be what they are. They would be shown as a random fluctuation of pricing. The third reason is that technical analysis assumes that history, as it usually does, will repeat itself. If similar conditions occurred in the past and are repeated in the present, it is quite likely that the same thing will occur in the future as well. Because individuals are not supposed to change in this equation, the second obvious conclusion is that their outcomes will be the same as well. In a nutshell, this was the basis of technical analysis. Don't forget that one of the most effective methods to improve your trading skills and raise your chances of being a successful investor is to be able to employ most of the information provided by this study.

There are a few counter-arguments against the use of technical analysis. Still, the only evidence you really need is that this analysis works and, at the very least, it may boost your odds of making more money when trading. We shall, however, highlight some of the attitudes toward technical analysis:

"Charts only indicate what has occurred in the past; how can they reflect what hasn't happened yet?" remarked one of the dealers. The explanation is simple: there is evidence from previous transactions, and that data is utilized in the technical analysis under the assumption that history will repeat itself. In this manner, you can forecast with some degree of precision. What is the next step in the market's price movement? In contrast, it works similarly to the weather prediction; if they say it will rain on TV, you know it may not rain even though they said it would, but you bring your umbrella nonetheless. The same approach applies to technical analysis, which is how you may anticipate the future by analyzing previous occurrences.

"If the prices already contain all there is to know, then any change in price can only come from fresh information that we don't currently know," said another dealer. This kind of concept may be seen in all financial markets, not only trading options. It appears in a variety of contexts, and scholars are currently debating it.

In contrast to a widespread belief among traders, this idea does not truly state that the current market price is right. It simply indicates that it is impossible to determine if the present price is too low or too expensive. As a result, the best method to deal with this topic is to demonstrate how technical analysis really works. Finally, if everyone agreed on this concept, we would have no analysis and the price would always be the same. We may conclude that technical analysis has self-fulfilling properties.

This implies that if the majority of traders do their research and believe that the price must rise, they will all become buyers on the market, resulting in an increase in demand and, as a result, a price increase. The same logic applies to the price that is expected to fall. This is yet another instance when technical analysis demonstrated that it works. Of course, there will always be some uncertainties, but does it really essential to show why the price moved in the manner you predicted? Furthermore, if a significant number of traders who are not highly informed and just want to make a fast profit fail, it may be taken as proof that the premise of having a huge number of traders regardless of their expertise and devotion is flawed from the start.

CHAPITRE 15:

‘

THE GREEKS

Trying to predict what will happen to the price of a specific option or a situation involving numerous choices as the market moves may be difficult. Understanding contributing elements to an option price's movement and the accompanying impacts is an important ability in options trading since the price of an option is not always driven by the price of the underlying asset.

Identifying the Values

To begin, bear in mind that the numbers allocated to Greeks are just speculative. These numbers are computed using mathematical models. The majority of the information needed to trade options, such as open interest, volume, latest prices, ask, and bid, is derived from facts obtained from various options exchanges and given by the brokerage business and/or data provider.

Greeks should be calculated, and their correctness is strongly reliant on the model employed to compute them. Obtaining them necessitates access to computerized solutions that calculate them based on your request. Most interactive brokers and retail brokerages provide this information as well. However, given the time limits and the number of accessible possibilities, learning the underlying arithmetic and manual computing for the Greeks is impractical and impossible.

The Delta's

Most newcomers to options trading believe that if a stock changes by a dollar, the options price based on it will move by more than a dollar. When you think about it, this notion is really absurd. Remember that the option is always priced cheaper than the stock, thus there is no logical reason to get a greater benefit than just holding the shares.

It is critical to have reasonable assumptions about the price behaviors of the traded options. The actual issue now is, if the price of a stock rises by $1, how much will the price of that option move?

This is when the term 'delta' comes into play.

Calls have a positive delta, which ranges between zero and one. As a result, when the price of a stock rises and no other pricing factors change, the call's price rises as well. For example, if a call has a delta of 0.50 and the stock rises by $1, the call's price should rise by around $0.50 as well.

As a general rule, 'in the money options will always move more than 'out of the money options. Furthermore, short-term options always respond more strongly to the same stock price shift than longer-term options.

As the expiry date approaches, the delta value for 'in the money puts approaches -1, whereas the delta value for 'out of the money options approaches 0. Because puts are locked until expiry, the owner must either exercise the options and sell the shares, or the put becomes worthless when it expires.

Different Ways of Viewing Delta

Delta's textbook definition is what we have already discussed.

However, you may consider delta in a different but important way: the likelihood that an option will expire at least $0.01 'in the money'.

Because the math underlying it is not considered normal probability computation, this may not be a genuine technical definition of delta. However, in the field of options trading, the delta is often utilized in conjunction with probability.

Dropping the decimal point in delta numbers is frequent in informal options trading jargon. As a result, you could hear someone remark, "That guy's option has a delta of 60." 'When I complete this e-book, there's a 99 percent chance I'll treat myself to a drink,' for example.

A call option that is at the money will often have a delta of roughly 0.50, or simply a '50 delta'. This is due to the fact that there is a 50/50 possibility that this option will be 'in the money' or 'out of the money' when it expires.

Now consider how the delta value changes when the option moves farther 'in the money' or 'out of the money'.

The Effect of Stock Price Movement on Delta

As an option becomes more 'in the money,' the likelihood that it will remain 'in the money' until it expires grows. As a result, the option's delta grows. As the option moves more 'out of the money,' the likelihood that it will end up 'in the money' when it expires reduces. As a result, the option's delta will decrease.

For example, suppose you hold a call option on stock ABC with a strike price of $50 and the stock price is $50 60 days before expiry. The delta is roughly 0.50 since this is an at-the-money option. Let's assume your choice costs $2. In theory, when the stock price rises to $51, the option price rises to $2.50, up from the initial $2.

What if the price of this stock rises from $51 to $52? The likelihood that the option will be 'in the money' when it expires has also increased. So, what becomes of Delta? You are accurate if you believe that the delta grows.

Let us provide an example to demonstrate the idea. If the stock price rises to $52 from $51, the option price may rise to $3.10 from $2.50, representing a $0.60 increase for every $1 rise in the stock price. This indicates that the delta grew from 0.50 to 0.60 ($3.10 minus $2.50 = $0.60) as the stock moved farther 'in the money'.

But what if, instead of rising, the stock price falls to $49 from $50? The option price may also fall from $2 to $1.50, reflecting the delta of 0.50 for 'at the money options' ($2 minus $1.50 = $0.50). However, if the stock price falls further to $48, the option price might fall to $1.10 from $1.50. In this situation, the delta was reduced to 0.40 ($1.50 less $1.10 = $0.40). This drop in delta indicates that the option's chances of being 'in the money' when it expires are likewise reduced.

How Delta Changes as Expiration Approaches

The time to expiry affects the possibility that options will be 'in the money' or 'out of the money,' much like the stock price. This is because, as the expiry date approaches, there is less time for the stock to go below or above the option's strike price.

Delta responds differently to stock price fluctuations because probability varies as expiry approaches. If the calls are 'in the money' right before expiry, the delta will approach 1 and the option will move penny-for-penny with the stock. Puts that are 'in the money', on the other hand, will approach -1 as expiry approaches.

If the option is 'out of money,' it will approach zero quicker than it would with greater time. It will also cease responding to the movement of the stock.

Let's look at another example from previously. You have stock ABC valued at $50, and the call option with a strike price of $50 is about to expire. The data is, as usual, around 0.50 since the stock has a theoretical 50/50 probability of moving in either direction. What happens if the stock rises to $51?

Consider the following situation. If the expiry date is just a day away and the option is a point 'in the money,' what is the likelihood that the option will stay at least $0.01 'in the money' tomorrow? You are accurate if you believe that is rather high. This is due to the delta increasing proportionally, resulting in a large jump to 0.90 from 0.50. Conversely, when stock ABC drops down to $49 from $50 a single day before the expiration date of the option, the delta can go down to 0.10 from 0.50, because of the lower possibility the option ends up 'in the money'.

As expiry approaches, changes in stock value will create more substantial changes in the delta due to the reduced or increased possibility of ending up 'in the money'.

Delta's Final Thoughts

Gamma

Delta represents speed, whereas gamma represents acceleration. Remember this comparison to better comprehend gamma and its relationship to the delta.

Gamma is defined as the rate at which the delta changes in response to a $1 change in the stock price. Options with a high gamma react the most to changes in the underlying stock's price.

The delta is a fluctuating number that fluctuates in tandem with the stock price. However, the delta does not always alter in response to the same rate of each option depending on a certain stock. Let's return to our stock ABC example with a $50 strike price to see how gamma changes in delta as the stock price changes and the time before it expires.

Look at the table above and see how gamma and delta vary when the stock price moves north and south beginning at $50, with the option moving 'in the money' or 'out of the money'. Given a comparable expiry, you will see that the 'at the money' options price changes more significantly than the 'in the money' or 'out of the money options price. Furthermore, near-term 'in the money option prices fluctuate more strongly than longer-term 'at the money' option prices. This gamma discussion demonstrates that near-term 'at money options prices will exhibit the most dramatic reaction to stock price fluctuations.

Theta

Theta, commonly known as time decay, is the option buyer's worst adversary. Theta, on the other hand, is the seller's best buddy. Theta is defined as the amount that puts and calls prices to reduce hypothetically for a one-day shift inside the expiry period.

The graph above depicts how the value of an option that is at the money will depreciate over the next three months until it expires. Take note of how the time value falls at a faster pace as expiry approaches. Time in the options market is analogous to the impact of summer heat on an ice cube. The temporal worth of the selection diminishes with each passing instant. And it does not dissolve in a linear value. As the expiry date approaches, the pace of this decline accelerates.

Looking at the graph again, you can see that a 90-day option that is at the money and has a $1.70 premium would lose $0.30 after 30 days. However, if the option has a 60-day expiry date, its value may decline by $0.40 after 30 days. The 30-day option, on the other hand, will lose its whole lifetime value of $1 when it expires.

Vega

Vega is seen by traders as the overly enthusiastic Greek in the bunch. It is defined as the amount put and call prices will move hypothetically for one implied volatility point shift. Vega has no effect on the inherent values of the options. It solely impacts the 'time value' of an option's price. When implied volatility rises, the value of options rises as well, since rising implied volatility suggests a wider range of probable market movement.

Rho, how about you?

Veteran option traders discuss another Greek - rho. It is defined as the amount by which the value of an option will change hypothetically if interest rates move by one percentage point.

However, as previously said, this Greek is intended for more experienced traders. You could get to meet him if you play this game long enough.

CHAPTER 16

OPTIONS TRADING TOOLS AND RULES

OPTION TRADING INSTRUMENTS

Stash: The finest app for novice traders to make investing choices. It is a trading and investing application. This is the best option for your requirements. Stash costs $5 to begin investing, provides advice on what to invest in, and provides more information on your assets. The app also includes important articles and ideas to help you enhance your investing expertise. Your money is invested in individual equities and ETFs that are part of several investing themes. Stash also includes an investing counselor.

Stockpile: You will be able to purchase and sell stocks using Stockpile. You may also donate single shares or purchase a portion of the shares for a minimum of 99 cents in trading costs. Using your account, you may use fractional transactions to acquire high-valued equities such as Google and Amazon. You will also not have to spend $1,000 or more for each share. You will also have the option of purchasing a piece of the stock to reduce the cost of your investment. Because of the ability to purchase and give stock shares, Stockpile is ideal for families.

Children, teens, and the whole family may have portfolios and educate your family on the value of investing, and this can become a family pastime. Teach your children about money and investing at a young age, and purchase or give them stocks. They will be able to develop a valuable portfolio by engaging them.

Schwab, Charles: The software allows you to manage your investments as well as your bank accounts all in one place. Schwab also offers the ability to transfer cash, deposit checks, and manage your accounts. You may also purchase and sell stocks, ETFs, and mutual funds. Schwab is popular among foreign travelers since it provides a checking ATM card with no additional costs wherever they travel.

Schwab is simple to use; you may access your assets from any Android, Apple, or Kindle Fire smartphone. The software also allows you to pay bills.

TD Ameritrade: The software is incredibly user-friendly and simple to use. It is appropriate for beginning option traders. TD Ameritrade provides customer service by phone and email 24 hours a day, seven days a week. The customer may also visit one of their numerous local locations for help, and the service can do research for them.

There are no hidden costs or platform fees with TD Ameritrade, and there is no minimum trading fee. The app charges a fixed fee of $6.95 for each equities trading and $0.75 per contract.

Mobile TradeStation: This app has a good rating and is available for free to all TradeStation customers. Users may see several option contracts with varying pricing and expiry dates. The TradeStation app provides traders with up-to-date information, as well as the ability to do options analysis and see charts with numerous technical indicators. The program has alerting tools, and traders may track price fluctuations and other indicators.

TradeStation is a full-service trading program that allows you to trade stocks, futures options, and FX.

Option Trading Regulations

What are the rules to follow while trading options? What are the guidelines? These are critical questions that rookie traders should be able to appropriately answer. In this book, we will go through the regulations that you should follow while trading options. And at the conclusion of this subject, you will have acquired the knowledge required to trade effectively. These regulations will be eye-opening for a new emerging trader, while they will serve as a reminder for a seasoned options trader. These are not get-rich-quick tips, but they will help you keep out of problems, build your wealth, and better your money with alternatives. Here are some of the options trading rules:

1. Start with tiny positions. When you enter the market, it's natural to expect the worst. To limit the danger of losing a considerable amount of money, it only makes sense to execute smaller transactions and avoid large trades.

The greatest advice is to open several little positions since if you open just one huge account, you risk getting knocked out when you lose. Because they trade big position sizes, over 90% of options traders fail. Trading more than 5% is considered a significant stake, and the trader risks having their accounts affected by a severe loss.

2. Avoid becoming emotional. The market doesn't care what you believe; one approach to be effective in trading is to stay emotionally detached. Allow your emotions, views, or ideas about the market to guide you.

3. Have a large number of trades. You will make a lot of trades if you know your projected % likelihood of success.

The more trades there are, the more likely it is that the proportion will level off. Options trading is a number game and a math game, and you can predict your chances of success in a certain position. You may see your success %; nevertheless, this might be the reason for your failure since you will have the same expectation in all of your transactions. As a result, the more trades you make, the more stable your % success rate will be.

4. Maintain a balanced portfolio. When you invest in options trading, you may wager on whether the price will rise or fall. Traders prefer to concentrate on rising investment values; nevertheless, you must also understand how to balance your portfolio with declining holdings.

5. Trade according to your degree of comfort. If you are uncomfortable trading naked options or if hedged positions give you nightmares, you should trade options as a speculator establishing views and acting on them.

When you are in sync with your tactics, you will notice that it is a lot simpler to earn money. Each technique is unique and special, and it may not be suitable for all traders. You will reduce the individual's danger level by doing so.

6. Always use a model. One of the most common errors option traders do is failing to assess the fair value of the option before selling or buying it. It may be difficult, particularly if you lack precise real-time assessment capacity. These are the foundations of strategic investment, and you should also be aware of the discounts and the price you are paying for the choice.

7. Maintain a sufficient cash reserve. It is critical to keep a large portion of your investment funds in cash. It might be handy for brokers that impose a margin requirement while trading. They allocate some funds to offset any losses on your stake. Attempt to retain 50-60% of your investment portfolio in cash.

8. Cut down on commissions and fees. Paying commissions and fees to trade and rebalance your portfolio may be financially ruinous. Using low-cost ETFs is one strategy to reduce the proportion of expenses. However, as a novice, you should not pay any fees while investing in stocks.

Ten Option Trading Commandments

One benefit of options trading is that you only lose the amount you paid for the options. However, no loss, no matter how little, is enjoyable. One of the most important aspects of generating money and becoming more successful in options trading is the ability to handle a loss. Here are 10 options trading commandments to assist you improve your options trading in the market:

1. Begin with little purchases. It is not advisable to engage in large option strategies if you have just begun trading in derivatives.

Begin with basic transactions such as purchasing and selling stock futures. As you gain expertise with these fundamental future transactions, you will gradually begin purchasing call-and-put options. To begin writing a call and putting options, you must be a knowledgeable investor.

2. Recognize the advantages. Examine the future and possibilities with a clear mind. If you trade short in the cash market, you must close your position that day.

However, if it is the future, you may continue in the short position until it expires.

3. Loss stops are required. Most traders lose their positions and never use the advised stop loss. When you use stop losses, you restrict your losses if the market moves against you. Any investor who enters the Options market should adhere to the stated stop loss.

4. The brokerage fallacy. Low brokerage fees may not necessarily result in huge returns. However, inexpensive services have low-quality suggestions, which leads to poor returns over time. The ideas with extensive research are of high quality. The exceptional quality is costly, with a high brokerage, but it is worthwhile since it will provide significant profits in the long run.

5. Don't be afraid to admit defeat. When an investor suffers a loss in the market, it is natural for them to panic. However, the options market provides enough flexibility to assist you in most cases. The market is volatile by nature, but having a knowledgeable adviser may help you lessen the danger of losing your investment. Here are some pointers to help option traders manage their emotions:

The big picture is to be aware of the macroeconomic environment and to avoid expensive assets.

Always have a trading strategy in place to avoid any emotions while purchasing or selling.

Prefer deals - instead of overpaying, search for cheap prices.

6. Profit is defined as what you book. Most investors get greedy in the market, particularly in F&O. It is critical that investors avoid being too greedy and record gains when they attain their desired return. It is better to book earnings twice than to wait too long. Your profit is determined by what you book in the market.

7. Guaranteed return has died. In the Options market, investors should avoid hoping for a guaranteed return. It is critical to recognize that the options market provides the benefits of the cash market with additional perks, but it is not a risk-free product.

8. Stick to a single trading strategy. Each brokerage firm follows and has its own research methodologies, which range greatly from one another. To earn a consistent return, an investor should remain with one brokerage firm.

9. Become acquainted with the terminology. Trading options without understanding the terminology is like piloting an aircraft without reading the instruments. There are significant insights accessible regarding the sensitivity of option costs to changes in the underlying shares, making it critical in risk management. An options trader should aim to get acquainted with the basic words employed, such as:

Delta: This is a measure of the rate of change in relation to the stock's cost rate. Consider the price value.

Vega: This gauge how sensitive options are to volatility, such as the volatility value.

Theta: This quantifies the sensitivity of options over a given time period, often known as the option's time decay, such as a time value.

10. Plan the transaction, then execute it. The disposition effect occurs when investors sell their gains too soon and hold their losses too long; this is quite prevalent. The reasons for the outcomes are unknown, but options traders may avoid this by developing a strategy before beginning trading and sticking to it.

Here are some actions you may take in order to prepare and execute trades:

CHAPITRE 17:

SUCCESSFUL TIPS

Know when to deviate from the script: While adhering to your strategy, even when your emotions urge you to disregard it, is a sign of a good trader, this does not imply that you must follow your plan 100% of the time. Without a doubt, you will sometimes find yourself in a scenario where your strategy is made entirely worthless by something beyond your control. You must be aware of your plan's flaws as well as changing market circumstances to recognize when pursuing your preset course of action will result in failure rather than success. Knowing when the situation is really changing vs when your emotions are attempting to take over is something that takes effort, but simply being aware of the difference is a significant step in the right direction.

Avoid out-of-the-money trades: While there are a few techniques out there that make a point of picking up options that are presently out of the money, you can be confident that they are the exception, not the norm. Remember that the options market is not like the conventional stock market, so buying cheap and selling high is not a realistic approach even if you are trading options based on underlying equities. If a call has dropped out of the money, there is generally less than a 10% chance that it will return to acceptable levels before it expires, which means that purchasing these types of options is a little better than gambling, and there are ways to gamble with odds much higher than 10% in your favor.

Avoid clinging to your first plan too tightly: Your basic trading strategy should be continually developing as the conditions around your trading habits alter and evolve. Furthermore, in addition to your major strategy, you will want to develop secondary plans that are more carefully targeted to certain market states or specialized tactics that are only helpful in a small range of conditions. Remember, the better prepared you are before beginning a trading day, the higher your total profit level is going to be, it's that easy.

Make use of the spread: If you are not completely risk averse, then when it comes to taking advantage of unpredictable transactions, the best thing to do is use a spread to both protect your current assets and profit. To use a long spread, create a call and a put with the same underlying asset, expiry information, and share quantities but two drastically different strike prices. The call must have a greater strike price to represent the upper limit of your earnings, while the put must have a lower strike price to represent the lower limit of your losses. It is critical to acquire both halves of a spread at the same time since doing so in fits and spurts might introduce unnecessary factors into the formula that are difficult to adjust for appropriately.

Never continue without first determining the market's mood: While employing a customized trading strategy is always the best option, having one does not alter the fact that it is critical to assess the market's mood before proceeding with the day's transactions.

First and foremost, it is important to remember that the collective desire of all traders now engaged in the market is just as powerful as anything more specific, including market news. For instance, even if corporations disclose positive news to numerous venues and the news is not as fantastic as everyone expected, associated prices might still fall.

To obtain a solid sense of the market's present attitude, you should be aware of the typical daily statistics that are prevalent in your market and keep an eye out for them to begin lowering quickly. While a day or two of considerable volatility is typical, anything more than that is a solid indicator that something is wrong. Furthermore, you should constantly be informed of what the top companies in your industry are up to.

Never begin without a defined entrance and departure strategy: While determining your initial set of entry/exit points without experience might be tough, it is critical that you have them nailed down before you begin trading, especially if the stakes are minor. Unless you are extraordinarily fortunate, beginning without a good understanding of the playing field will result in you losing money. If you're not sure what limitations to establish, start with a broad pair of points and work your way down from there.

More crucial than establishing entrance and departure points, however, is employing them even when there seems to be money on the table.

One of the most difficult obstacles for inexperienced options traders to overcome is the belief that you must squeeze every last penny out of every good deal. The truth is that as long as you have a profitable trading strategy, there will always be more profitable trades in the future, which means that rather than worrying about a small extra profit, you should be more concerned with protecting the profit that the trade has already netted you. While disregarding this advice may sometimes result in little profit, the chances are that you will lose considerably more than you gain when earnings peak abruptly and begin to fall again before you can successfully pull the trigger.

If you're still having trouble grasping this notion, examine this:

Options trading is a marathon, not a sprint; slow and steady wins the race every time.

Never, ever double down: Many new options traders will find themselves in a situation where the best way to recoup a significant loss is to double down on the underlying stock in question at its newest, significantly lowered, price in an attempt to make a profit under the assumption that things will turn around and then continue to do so until everything is completely profitable once again. While it might be tough to let an underlying stock that was once incredibly lucrative go, doubling down is almost never a good idea. whether you find yourself in a scenario where you are unsure if the transaction you are about to make is a good one, just ask yourself whether you would make the same one if you were going into the situation blind. The answer should tell you all you need to know.

If you find yourself in a scenario where doubling down seems to be the best option, you will need the fortitude to talk yourself back down from that investment ledge and to reduce your losses as comprehensively as feasible given the present circumstances. The sooner you cut your losses and move on from a losing trade, the sooner you may start investing your efforts and investments into a transaction that still has the potential to bring you money.

Nothing should ever be taken personally: It is the human propensity to create tales about, and so establish connections with, inanimate things such as particular stocks or currency pairings. This is why it is absolutely reasonable to develop a stronger attachment to certain trades and even contemplate abandoning your strategy if one of them takes an unexpected plunge. However, thinking about and acting on are two very different things, which is why being aware of these inclinations is critical in order to avoid them at all costs.

This situation occurs just as often with good transactions as it does with negative ones, but the outcomes are always the same. In particular, it may be highly tempting to hold on to a certain transaction for much longer than you would otherwise decide to just because it is on a hot run that shows no signs of abating. In these cases, the ideal course of action is to sell half of your shares and then establish a new goal based on the revised facts to guarantee you can have your cake and eat it too.

Not taking your broker's recommendation seriously: With so many factors to consider, it's easy to see why many inexperienced options traders just choose the first broker they come across and start trading. The reality of the matter is, however, that the broker you pick will be a significant part of your entire trading experience, so choosing the proper one should not be underestimated if you want the greatest experience possible. This implies that the first thing you need does is look beyond the welcoming façade of their website and get to the meat and potatoes of what they genuinely provide.

Remember that although developing an eye-catching website is simple, populating it with real material while having malicious intent is far more difficult.

First and foremost, this entails investigating their customer service history to ensure not only that they treat their consumers properly, but also that the quality of service is where it should be. Remember that when you make a deal, every second counts, therefore if you need to call your broker for assistance with a trade, you need to know that you will be speaking with someone who can fix your issue as soon as possible. Giving them a call and seeing how long it takes for them to come back to you is the best method to ensure their customer service is up to par. If you have to wait more than one business day, take your business somewhere because if they are this uninterested in a new customer, imagine what the service will be like after they already have you where they want you.

With that out of the way, the next item to consider is the costs that the broker will collect in return for their services.

There is virtually little control when it comes to these fees, so it will absolutely pay to shop around. In addition to costs, it is critical to evaluate any mandatory account minimums as well as any fees associated with removing money from the account.

Locate a Mentor: When it comes to progressing from a casual trader to someone who trades effectively regularly, there is only so much you can learn on your own before you need a really impartial eye to verify you are on the right track. This individual might be someone you know in real life or one or more persons you've met online. The objective is that you need to locate another individual or two with whom you can bounce ideas and gain expertise. Options trading does not have to be a lonely pastime; join any community you can discover.

CHAPTER 18

TOP TRADER MISTAKES

Options trading is a whole different beast than traditional stock market investment. Consider the prevalent knowledge that is disseminated about stock market investment for a minute. The fundamental concept is to acquire and retain your assets for an extended length of time. In fact, you are supposed to hold your assets until retirement. People use numerous tactics like portfolio rebalancing to meet their objectives, diversification, and dollar-cost averaging.

Trading options is a very new way of looking at things. To begin with, whether you are a day trader or engage in swing trading, the overall aim when it comes to stocks is to purchase when the price is relatively low and then sell when the price is relatively high. In actuality, day traders, swing traders, and buy-and-hold investors are all the same. Buy-and-hold investors believe they are unique and superior to others, yet they are just attempting to profit from the stock market. Unless you are a dividend investor, the only significant difference is the time length involved. So, your buy-and-hold investor will retain the stocks for 25 years before cashing them out for cash. A swing trader earns money in the present.

In that way, options trading is similar to swing trading. In reality, in many circumstances, you're seeking the same price fluctuations as a swing trader. However, as we have seen, options enable various methods that are not accessible to any other form of stock market participant.

In principle, you could acquire a large number of shares of stock and attempt to put up similar arrangements, but it would simply not work. Aside from that, even if it did, it would need a massive investment.

The purpose of this conversation is just to create the basis and realize that most of us approach possibilities with a totally different attitude. It does take some getting accustomed to, and many new options traders will make blunders. That's simply the way the market is since it's so different from what people are accustomed to.

We will look at some of the most co

mmon errors made by new options traders. There isn't a full list; I chose the ones that I've observed the majority of people make.

Entering a Large Trade

One of the pitfalls that many make when they first start trading options is taking up overly large bets. People aren't accustomed to investing in tiny sums since our options aren't very expensive in comparison to stock prices. Even those who are not wealthy are concerned with the stock price and the cost of 100 shares. This can get individuals into trouble. When you begin trading, the temptation will be to move on a big number of contracts if you have the funds to buy or sell them.

This may genuinely get folks in hot water. It's not so much the cash number as it is the fact that it may put you in a position where you're not ready to move as soon as you would need to depending on the scenario. So, if you uncover a trade and decide to sell 20 contracts, attempting to repurchase 20 contracts may be difficult if the transaction goes south. Or you might find yourself purchasing a number of call options and having difficulty getting rid of them all on the same day.

It is really preferable to have a few distinct tiny roles with possibilities rather than a vast number of positions. Keep in mind that option prices change quickly. You don't want to over-leverage your deals and end up unable to locate a buyer for all 10 or 20 contracts.

Failure to Pay Attention to the Expiration

This is most likely one of the most prevalent blunders made by new traders. One of the most crucial elements to consider when entering transactions is the expiry date. And after you've entered a deal, you must have the options' expiry dates tattooed on your forehead. This is not something that should be overlooked. To begin with, selecting the expiry date when entering the position is just as crucial as selecting the option's strike price. However, one of the mistakes that novices do is focusing too much on the option's price and the strike price. The cost of the option and the strike price are clearly crucial, but so is the expiry date.

Unfortunately, far too many new traders disregard the expiry date when their deals fail. As a result, they just let the option expire. Of course, if it occurs and you are out of money, you are completely out of luck. It will just be a total loss. So, before we join the trade, we must pay attention to expiry dates, and we must also pay attention to expiration dates when managing the deal.

Purchasing Low-Cost Options

You get what you paid for, as the phrase goes. There are instances when you should purchase out-of-the-money options, but you shouldn't go too far out of the money. Unfortunately, many new traders are tempted to trade far out of the money in order to get a low-priced option. The issue with these options is that, although out of the money, choices may profit. If they are too far out of pocket, they will simply not witness any activity. So, there's no use in purchasing a cheap choice simply because you can get it for $25. You don't want to put your money into options where a large price shift is required to generate any returns. It is OK to purchase options that are close to expiration.

Options that are close to being in the money may be highly rewarding even if they are not. So, if you want to save a little money when you first start investing, it is always something to think about. However, in order to benefit, there must be a fair likelihood that the stock prices will move enough to make the option you buy profitable.

When Selling Options, Failure to Close

If you just remember one thing from our explanation of selling options, whether it's selling put credit spreads or naked puts, bear in mind that you may always quit the transaction.

When you sell to open, you exit the deal by buying to close. You must be cautious since it is all too easy to give in to your emotions and fear, causing you to abandon a deal prematurely.

However, you must be mindful of the prospect of having to close the deal at any point. Riding out an option until it expires is a stupid action unless it is quite evident that it will expire out of the money.

As part of the issue, new options traders often enter the market and use hope as a tactic. When it comes to investing, hoping is not a plan. Hope is something that belongs in a casino where people play slot machines. When weighing your training alternatives, make the most logical conclusion you can give the conditions. So, as the expiry date approaches and it is evident that the trade will not be lucrative, resist the desire to wait for a reversal in direction. When you say things like that to yourself, you open yourself up to the temptation to remain in the trade for much too long. You may not be able to recover completely at some time. So, what you don't want to do, and this is true for both purchasing and selling, is hope for a reversal and then wait to see what occurs.

This is the worst of all potential methods for individuals who are purchasing options to open positions.

Remember that when you purchase to open a position, time decay is always working against you. So, unless the stock is trending upward, there is no need to retain the option. Time decay really works to your advantage as a seller.

However, there are times when it is just prudent to exit the transaction. Consider the following instances.

If you sell to open an iron condor and the stock breaks out in one way or the other, it's best to exit the iron condor immediately. We're not talking about a one- or two-dollar bill. If the market moves in such a way that one of your options becomes profitable by a little margin, that sort of transaction is worth watching to see what occurs. However, if there is a significant break to the upside or fall, it would be unwise to remain in the trade. For one thing, there is a chance of assignment, but the most probable scenario is that you will simply lose the greatest amount of money. However, if you have a sound strategy and only invest in options with a large amount of open interest, you should be able to purchase and sell that option very rapidly, regardless of the scenario.

Another apparent example is if you were selling a naked put credit spread and observed that the share price was falling straight near your strike price. You don't have to worry right immediately since, in order for exercising the option to be profitable, the share price must rise enough such that not only does the option go in the money, but the price movement also accounts for the money paid for the premium to acquire the contract. So, if you have a $100 strike price and someone pays two dollars for the option if the share price is $99, they will exercise the option. Even if it falls below $98, they may not exercise the option unless there is some indication that the stock is likely to turn around and they can sell it at a profit. However, it is an improbable case. It's only when it gets very hot that there's an issue.

Investing in Illiquid Options

I'll say it again since this is such an essential subject. When trading options, liquidity is critical. Liquidity refers to the capacity to promptly acquire and sell financial securities and convert them into cash. It is not enough to like the firm in order to begin trading options on it. If the open interest for an option is merely 8, 10, or even 45, it will create challenges when you need to act quickly to get rid of an option. The bigger corporations usually provide liquid choices, but you should always double-check. Index funds offer liquid choices as well. Avoid any corporations with minor open interests. The only reason you would trade when open interest is low is if the risk of losing the deal is negligible. So, in addition to the strike price, share price, and expiry date, you should pay particular attention to open interest. You don't want to be in a position where you can't get out.

CHAPTER 19

THE TOP 5 REASONS TRADERS LOSE MONEY

Put the following "5 Commandments" on a sticky note and adhere it to your computer screen:

Stocks nearing 52-week lows should not be purchased.

Avoid trading penny stocks.

Stocks should not be shorted.

Never trade on margin.

Don't exchange thoughts with others.

1. Avoid buying equities that have reached 52-week lows.

So many inexperienced traders lose a lot of money while attempting to catch the famous "falling knife." Contrary to popular belief, you are nearly always better off purchasing a stock that is reaching 52-week highs rather than one that is hitting 52-week lows.

Have you just received devastating news about a firm you own? If this is the case, keep in mind that there is never just one cockroach. The bad news arrives in waves. Many investors recently learned this the hard way when General Electric simply kept presenting bad news after terrible news, leading the stock to plummet from 30 to 7. There's no such thing as "safe stock." Even a blue-chip stock might plummet significantly if it loses its competitive edge if the firm makes poor judgments.

A chain reaction of unfavorable news may often lead a stock to trend down or gap down repeatedly. If you hold a stock that behaves in this manner, it is frequently wiser to exit and wait a few months (or years) before reentering. Once again, there is never a single cockroach.

Never purchase stock after seeing your first cockroach. When a stock falls dramatically, it might have an impact on the company's fundamentals. Employee and management morale may suffer, the best staff may quit, and raising funds via the sale of shares or the issuance of debt may become more difficult.

When a stock rises dramatically, it may strengthen the company's fundamentals. Employee and management morale will be high, everyone at the firm will want to work more, recruiting fresh talent will be easier, and the company will be able to borrow money more easily by issuing stock or debt.

Stick to equities that are trading above their 200-day moving averages or are nearing 52-week highs, and you will do far better than attempting to catch falling knives.

2. Avoid trading penny stocks.

A penny stock is any stock that trades for less than $5. All penny stocks should be avoided unless you are an experienced trader. I would go a step further and advise you to avoid any companies priced under $10.

Even if you have a tiny trading account ($5,000 or less), purchasing fewer shares of a higher-priced stock is preferable to buying a large number of shares of a penny stock.

This is due to the fact that low-priced stocks are sometimes linked with lower-quality enterprises. As a consequence, they are often not permitted to trade on the NYSE or the Nasdaq. Instead, they trade on the OTCBB ("over the counter bulletin board") or Pink Sheets, which have substantially laxer financial reporting standards than the main exchanges.

Many of these businesses have never turned a profit. They might be scams or shell firms set up primarily to benefit management and other insiders. They may also include former "blue chips" that have gone bankrupt, such as Eastman Kodak or Lehman Brothers.

Furthermore, penny stocks are more volatile than higher-priced equities. Consider this: if a $100 stock moves $1, that is a 1% move. A $1 move in a $5 stock is a 20% move. Many rookie traders misjudge the emotional and financial harm that such volatility may bring.

Penny stocks, in my experience, do not trend nearly as well as higher-priced ones. They are more mean reversing (Mean reversion happens when a stock rises substantially from its average trading price, only to fall back to its average trading price). Many of them will ultimately be zero, but they are not ideal short candidates. The majority of brokers will not allow you to short them.

Even if you do locate a broker that would let you short a penny stock, how would you want to wake up one morning to discover your penny stock trading at $10 when you just shorted it a few days before for $2? I had to learn the lesson the hard way. It turns out that I was risking $8 to earn $2, which is not a viable long-term strategy.

To add insult to injury, a penny stock may look to be liquid one day and then dry up the next, leaving you with a $2 bid/ask spread. Or the offer might just vanish.

Consider buying a stock for which there are now no buyers.

Avoid any stocks priced under $10. Avoid trading newsletters that promote penny stocks. The proprietors of these newsletters are often compensated by the firms themselves to promote their stocks. Or they may acquire a penny stock, send out an email asking everyone to buy it, and then sell their shares at a much higher price to these inexperienced buyers.

Watch the film "The Wolf of Wall Street" to witness a classic example of the lavish lifestyle and deception that often accompany penny stocks. Viewers should use caution.

3. Avoid shorting stocks.

If you are an experienced trader, you may disregard this guideline. If you are not, I strongly advise you not to break this rule.

To short a stock, you must first borrow shares of it from your broker. The shares are then sold on the open market. If the stock price declines, you will be able to repurchase those shares at a profit. However, if the stock rises significantly, you may be obliged to repurchase the shares at a much higher price, costing you more money than you had in your trading account, to begin with.

Joe Campbell violated two of the five commandments in November 2015.

He began by trading a penny stock named KaloBios Pharmaceuticals. To make matters worse, he decided to sell it short.

His trading account was valued at around $37,000 when he went to bed that evening. The stock had risen dramatically by the time he awoke the following morning. As a consequence, he not only lost the whole $37,000, but he also owed his broker an extra $106,000.

And there was no escape. If you owe money to your broker, they may take you to court and seize your home and savings.

Even the wealthiest investors may be wiped out by shorting a stock. Shares of the railroad stock rose from $170 to $1,000 in a single day during the Great Northern Pacific Corner of 1901. That maneuver bankrupted some of the country's richest citizens, who had shorted the stock and were then obliged to cover at higher prices.

If you do decide to short a stock, keep in mind that your broker will charge you a fee to borrow the shares (typically stated as an annual interest rate). Furthermore, if you are short a stock, you are responsible for paying any dividends on that stock (your broker will deduct the money from your account weekly).

Shorting stocks is obviously an advanced and hazardous trading method for all of these reasons. Don't do it unless you've been trading for at least 5 years and have the financial stability to sustain a stock's wild upward surge.

Also, never sell a penny stock short. It's just not worth it.

4. Avoid trading on margin.

To short a stock, you must first create a margin account with your broker, as Joe Campbell did. To trade stocks on margin, you'll also need a margin account. When you buy a stock on margin, you are borrowing money from your broker in order to acquire more shares of stock than you would ordinarily be able to buy with only the cash in your brokerage account.

Assume I have $10,000 in my margin account. Most brokers in the United States will enable me to buy $20,000 worth of stock on margin in that account. This implies that they are financing me an extra $10,000 (typically at an exorbitant yearly interest rate of 11%, which E*Trade now charges) to purchase more stock. If I invest $10,000 in stock and it rises 10%, I will have earned $1,000. But if I can use a margin loan to boost the amount of stock, I'm purchasing to $20,000, I'll have profited $2,000 on the same 10% rise. That means my trading account has increased by 20% ($2,000/$10,000).

Of course, if the stock falls 10% and I'm using full margin, I'll lose 20% of my account worth. Trading on margin is essentially a sort of leverage: it enhances your portfolio's performance on both the upside and downside. When you use margin to purchase a stock, the stock and cash in your trading account serve as security for the margin loan. If the stock falls enough, you may be obliged to instantly contribute additional cash to your account (this is known as "getting a margin call"), or risk having the broker force you to sell your shares to obtain cash. This often results in you selling the stock at the worst possible moment. When opening a new brokerage account and offering the option of a "cash account" or a "margin account," choose "margin account." A margin account provides several benefits, such as the ability to utilize the funds from a stock sale to quickly purchase another stock without having to wait a few days for the deal to settle. You will never be charged fees or interest if you never exceed your cash purchasing power in a margin account. In this approach, having a margin account but never going on margin is quite conceivable.

If you don't believe in yourself, start a "cash account." As a result, you will never be permitted to trade on margin.

5. Do not exchange thoughts with others.

This is due to two major factors.

The first reason you should never exchange someone else's ideas is that they most likely don't know what they're doing. If you receive a hot stock tip from a neighbor or at the gym, disregard it. They most likely have no clue what they're talking about. Second, even if you acquire a great and genuine trading or investment suggestion from someone else, you will most likely lack the confidence to stick with it when times become bad. That conviction can only come through establishing your own trade concept. You will have the conviction to hang on after you have planned a trade or investigated an investment for yourself. You'll also know where your stop loss is in case the stock falls. Have you ever noticed how popular stock picks never include a suggested stop loss level?

Also, never make a deal based on anything you just read in Barron's, Forbes, The Wall Street Journal, or saw on CNBC. Never purchase a stock on the basis of an analyst upgrade or sell a stock on the basis of an analyst downgrade.

DEBIT AND CREDIT SPREADS

CREDIT SPREAD ON PUTS

The goal of a put credit spread is to profit from the sale of a put option. To limit the risk, you purchase a put option at the same time. This is not the same as selling a naked put option when you just sell one option and that's it.

Because the option you purchase will reduce your risk somewhat, you are not subject to the same requirements as someone selling naked put options. However, in order to apply this approach, you must have a level 3 trading account.

The first thing to understand about the put credit spread is that you are selling in order to start the position. So, this is selling rather than purchasing to exchange options. There is a theoretical risk of assignment, but as we'll see, it's not a real danger in practice, and since the trade is offset by the second put that you purchase to initiate the trade, the actual effect is minor.

Because the two options are purchased and sold in the same transaction, this is considered a single trade rather than two independent deals. You may purchase a put debit spread, which means the opposite party to the transaction is doing so when you sell to open your position.

The premise behind this sort of trade is that you anticipate the stock price to remain roughly where it is today, only slightly declining in price, or slightly growing in price. Because it is a "bullish" move, it is often referred to as a bull credit spread, while the term put credit spread is significantly more accurate.

Second, it's not really a bullish move in the sense that you're expecting the stock price will skyrocket. If that occurs, you will undoubtedly be better off. If you put it up correctly, you will gain the maximum profit immediately away while still allowing some leeway for the stock to fall before the scene changes.

One of the distinctive aspects of a put credit spread that we have not observed in our options research is that once the price hits a specific level, that is it. A further rise in the share price will not boost our earnings. Consider the put credit spread for Amazon in the example below. When you sell to begin the position, you get a $4.92 credit to your account (100 shares x $492 total). The stock is now trading in the maximum gain zone. If the share price rose by $100, it would have little effect on the seller of this credit spread other than to relieve them that they would undoubtedly benefit from the sale.

So, although it seems to be a bullish strategy, what you are actually doing with a put credit spread is betting that the price does not decline. You are employing out-of-the-money put options to set up the trade, and the goal is that they will expire out-of-the-money, allowing you to pocket the net premium paid on the contract.

Debit Spread Put

If you believe the stock will fall but would rather purchase to establish a position, you might employ a put debit spread. This is similar to a call debit spread, except that you are betting on the share price falling. Losses are restricted to the expense of entering the position. Profits, however, are also limited. Limiting possible losses also limits potential rewards.

In this situation, you purchase a put at a strike price that you believe would be lucrative. You sell a put option at a lower strike price to minimize your overall risk and the amount you pay to start the position.

For example, we may enter a put debit spread on Facebook for a cost of $1.26 to initiate the position. In this case, the higher strike price is $192.50, thus we purchase this put option. Then, at a lower strike price, we sell a put option. It's $187.50 in this scenario.

The maximum loss is limited to the cost of entering the position, thus we may lose $126 per contract.

Breakeven is calculated as the higher strike price less the credit received, which in this example is $191.24.

When the share price falls below the lower strike price, the maximum profit is realized. In order to maximize earnings, Facebook's share price would have to fall to $187.50 or below.

That may happen after a terrible earnings call, but it's unlikely to happen under regular circumstances unless there's some very severe news. Of course, this does happen from time to time, but you should join trades like this with caution and without giving it much thought and preparation. Before going into a deal like this, you should have a good understanding of it.

Credit Spread on Calls

A call credit spread is similar to a put credit spread, except this is a transaction you would employ if you believe the stock price would fall. A sell-to-open position is a call credit spread. You earn by selling a call option and reducing prospective losses by purchasing a call option with the same expiration date but a different strike price. You sell a call with a lower strike price in this situation. Purchasing a call with a higher strike price reduces the risk.

The credit gained from selling the position is the maximum profit.

If the stock price rises over the lower strike price, you will begin to lose money. We'll use Facebook as an example to demonstrate how this works. The share price is $199.27. A call credit spread is formed by selling a call option with a strike price of $202.50 and purchasing a call option with a strike price of $210.

This transaction would result in a credit of $3.30, or $330 for all 100 shares. The breakeven point is simple to compute.

You do this by applying the lower strike price to the credit received:

$202.50 + $3.30 = $205.80.

The maximum profit is obtained as long as the share price remains below the lower strike price call, in this example, $202.50. That is the credit obtained, which is $330. Maximum loss happens if the share price climbs over the higher strike price call, therefore a $420 loss occurs if the share price increases above $210. The maximum loss is determined by the difference in strike prices less the credit obtained. In this scenario, $210 minus $202.50 minus $3.30 is $4.20.

Spread on Calls and Debits

A call debit spread is a strategy that is used when you believe the share price of a company will rise. To engage in a single transaction, you purchase a call option and sell a call option in this case. However, instead of receiving a net credit as with a put credit spread, you will get a net debit in this situation, indicating that this is a buy-to-open position.

The two options in a call debit spread have the same expiry date, and the spread is caused by the options having different strike prices. In this instance, you purchase a call with a lower strike price. The next step is to sell a call with a higher strike price. You gain credit for it, which reduces the amount paid on purchasing the lower strike price call. This will reduce the amount of profit possible from the deal. So, the profit is restricted, but the risk is also reduced since the call option you sell will partly balance any losses you receive from the call option you acquire. The profit is achieved in this situation by purchasing the call option with the lower strike price.

The premium paid to join the position determines the maximum loss that may be suffered when purchasing a call debit spread.

In this situation, breakeven is calculated as a lower call strike price + debit paid to join the position

You choose a strike price for the lower call that you believe will be beneficial. So, you're expecting that the share price will rise over the strike price. To maximize profits, the share price must equal or surpass the higher call strike price.

So, for example, we utilize Apple again. This time, we're going to purchase a call debit spread with a lower strike price of $217.50 and a higher strike price of $220. The maximum loss is incurred for any share price at expiry that is less than the bottom strike price of $217.50. The trade costs $0.54 to enter, hence the breakeven price is $217.50 + $0.54 = $218.04. To maximize profit, the share price must rise over the higher strike price, in this instance $220. The highest profit for this transaction is $196, and the greatest loss is the $54 credit paid to join the deal.

To be explicit, you would purchase the lower strike price call, i.e., the $217.50 call. Then you sell the higher strike price call, which in this case would be the $220 call option.

To demonstrate how the higher-priced call option reduces the cost of entry, purchase the $217.50 call alone for $1.64, for a total of $164. The highest money that may be lost while purchasing a call is the amount paid, which is $164. The greatest profit, on the other hand, is potentially infinite.

CHAPTER 21:

\

FOR BEGINNERS, HOW TO TRADE OPTIONS ON ROBINHOOD IN 2020

WHAT EXACTLY IS ROBINHOOD?

Simply described, Robinhood is a smartphone software for online stock brokerage. Robinhood is not like other stock trading programs such as E*TRADE or TD Ameritrade. The primary difference is that instead of charging a commission of 5-10 dollars for each transaction plus additional expenses, Robinhood allows you to make all of your trades for free. They never, ever charge you commissions or fees. This one basic distinction opens up a plethora of alternatives for ordinary people that were previously exclusively accessible to the affluent and wealthy.

Robinhood even offers free shares of companies such as Apple, Microsoft, Ford, and Sirius XM Radio in exchange for installing their app.

When and Why Should You Use Robinhood?

Robinhood is still in its early stages. You don't receive the advantages of having your stocks in an IRA or Roth IRA when you use their app. I wouldn't use it to save your life money. What Robinhood is fantastic for is beginning a stock portfolio from nothing and growing it as cheaply as possible to huge sums that can subsequently be transferred to an IRA or Roth IRA for long-term advantages. In this series, we will use Robinhood to make more short-term trades with the objective of maximum gain in fewer than five years.

Installing the app and receiving your first free share of stock

Just for installing the app and creating an account, Robinhood will offer you a free share of stock. The accounts are completely free to open, so there is no cost to you. All you have to do is use a referral link like this one to download the app. CLICK HERE TO GET THE ROBINHOOD APP AND YOUR FIRST FREE STOCK. To establish an account, you must provide your name and contact information. Then, from the menu, choose Free Stocks. On this page, look for the PAST INVITES link in the upper right corner. To get your free stock, follow this link. A list of all the free stocks you get may also be seen here. For each person you suggest who uses the Robinhood app, you will get one free share of a stock chosen at random from their inventory. Our tactics for acquiring a lot of referrals (and free stocks) will be found in the next book in our series Tons of Free Stocks on Robinhood.

Search and Watchlist features

Robinhood, like any other stock trading platform, includes a watch list that allows you to follow the price changes of your favorite companies. It includes some of the most popular stocks, like Facebook, Apple, Google, and Amazon. While you may trade these stocks on Robinhood, they are rather pricey, ranging from $100 to $1000. We'll use the search option to locate stocks that are cheaper for beginners and add them to our watchlist. Robinhood does not recommend stocks to purchase and does not have a comprehensive list of all accessible stocks. So, in terms of discovering stocks to purchase, you're pretty much on your own.

You may use Google to search for stock tips and similar terms to locate firms that are anticipated to rise in value and get the symbols for such companies, such as Facebook (FB) and Apple (AAPL). Once you've found the symbol for a firm you like, open the Robinhood app and tap the magnifying glass in the upper right corner. Enter the symbol you discovered, and the firm will appear. From here, you'll see a little circle with a + sign within. You may add a firm to your watchlist by clicking on this icon. Alternatively, you may click on the business name to learn more about the stock, such as its price, volume, average volume, market capitalization, dividend ratios, and so on.

Purchasing your first stock

I'm sure you're eager to start buying and selling stocks for a profit by now. I recommend that you start small and work your way up. Add stock to your watchlist that you can afford. Click on the stock you wish to purchase on your watchlist, and the details page will appear.

There is a button at the bottom of the page that says trade or purchase.

To begin the purchase order, click this button. Robinhood will instantly launch the market order form. Enter the number of shares you wish to purchase and click Send. You should be aware that when utilizing a market order, Robinhood may acquire the stock at a price that is up to 5% higher than the current market price. A limit order is used to purchase stocks at a particular price. By clicking on the link in the upper right corner of the trading screen, you may alter the order type.

Limit and market orders what do they serve?

Market orders basically tell Robinhood that you want to sell this stock at whatever the market price is, regardless of whether it moves up or down.

If you place a buy order, Robinhood will automatically acquire available shares at up to 5% over the current market price.

Anything greater than 5% will result in the order being canceled. If you put in a sell order, it will sell at the current market price, even if it lowers swiftly.

A limit order informs Robinhood that you want to sell this stock but only at a specified price. If you change the order type to a limit order by clicking the link in the upper right corner of the trading screen, Robinhood will ask you to input the precise price you are going to pay for that stock and will only fulfill the order if it is available at that price or below. If you're selling, you'll be asked to enter the minimum amount you're willing to sell for, and the transaction will only be completed if the price hits that level or above.

Orders for stop loss and stop limit what do they serve?

A stop-loss order instructs the seller to sell a stock if it reaches a specified price. This is your safety net, and we'll be utilizing it often later in our course to reduce danger. When you change your order type to this, you will be asked to specify a price. If you are buying, enter the price you wish to pay and your order will be converted to an order when the stock hits that price or greater. If you are selling, you should set a price so that if the stock price goes below that level, your order will be converted to an order. This is beneficial since it enables you to build up a safety net so you don't have to continually monitor your stocks to prevent a loss.

For example, suppose you pay $5.00 for a stock. You place a sell-stop order if the price goes below $4.95. If the price rises, you will continue to profit from the stock. If the price goes below $4.95, your order will be converted to an order and the stock will be sold to prevent additional losses.

A stop limit order is an order to sell a stock at a certain price.

However, when the stock reaches that level, it will convert to a limit order. A stop-limit order must have two price points. One pricing point is for converting the order and another for limiting an order.

This enables you to form a vehicle through which to purchase the shares. For example, you believe that if a certain stock breaks beyond its 52-week high, it will get a boost from many individuals anticipating that it will continue to rise. However, after the first wave of purchasers has passed, the volume will return to normal, falling slightly before gradually rising again.

Assume the stock is worth $8 per share. The 52-week high per share is $10. You enter a stop limit order with a convert price of $10 per share and a limit price of $15 per share. At the end of the day, a huge hedge fund decides to acquire the stock and makes a massive order for millions of shares. In after-hours trading, the stock soars to $20.

Because you're using a free account, your orders cannot be executed aftermarket hours. When the markets open in the morning, the large players have already finished their orders. The price remains at $20, but it begins to fall since no small investors are ready to pay such a high amount. If you had utilized a stop-loss order, you would have bought the stock at a high price and subsequently sold it at a lower price.

However, if you use a stop-limit order, you will not acquire any shares till the price falls below $15.

CHAPTER 22

EXOTIC ALTERNATIVES

An exotic option has a fundamental structure that varies from either European or American options in terms of how and when the payoff will be made, as well as how the option connects to the underlying asset in the issue. Furthermore, the number of possible underlying assets will be much greater and might include things like what the weather is like or how much rainfall a certain location has received. Exotic options are exclusively traded over the counter due to their customization choices and complexity.

While exotic alternatives are obviously more difficult to become engaged with, they also provide various extra benefits when compared to regular options, including:

They are a superior option for individuals that have particularly precise risk management requirements.

When it comes to risk management and trading, they provide a range of distinct risk dimensions.

They provide a far broader choice of prospective investments that may more readily suit the demands of a diversified range of portfolios.

They are often less expensive than standard choices.

They also have several disadvantages, the most significant of which is that they are often not priced accurately using normal pricing formulae. This might be a profit rather than a disadvantage, depending on whether the mispricing benefits the trader or the writer. It is also vital to remember that the degree of risk involved with exotic options is always going to be higher than with ordinary options owing to the restricted liquidity available for each form of exotic option. While some varieties may have extremely active marketplaces, others will just have a limited amount of interest. Some are even dual-party transactions, which means they have no underlying liquidity and are only exchanged when two willing traders are located.

There are several unusual variations available, including:

Choose an option: The most frequent exotic option is the chosen option, which enables the investor to choose whether the option is a call or a put at various periods throughout the option's lifecycle. Because this option might change throughout the holding period, it is not listed on any normal exchange.

A barrier option is a form of option whose payoff varies based on whether the underlying asset has reached a certain price. A barrier option may also be a knock-out option, which implies it will expire at $0 if the underlying asset likewise climbs over a certain price. This reduces the holder's earnings while protecting the writer's assets fairly well. On the contrary, it might be a knock-in, which implies it will have no value until the underlying asset hits a certain price threshold.

Because of their intricacy, barrier options are regarded as exotic choices. They are also classified because they are a path-dependent option, and their value is reliant on the value fluctuations of the underlying asset throughout the course of its life.

Essentially, this implies that the payment from these options is determined by the asset's price path rather than its actual price.

An Asian option is one that pays out depending on the underlying asset's average price over a predetermined period of time rather than when it reaches maturity. This form of option appeals to certain traders since it might assist to safeguard them during a time of significant market volatility. It is seen as an exotic alternative since it is less expensive than the conventional American option.

A digital option is a form of option with a set payment that pays out if the underlying stock hits or surpasses a certain strike price. A digital option is similar to a binary option, except that it only applies to stock options. If the notion that inspired it comes true, the option will be automatically exercised. They are also distinct from typical binary options in that they are often traded on unregulated sites. This implies they have a greater overall risk of being involved in fraudulent activities.

Compound options: A compound option is a sort of option in which another option serves as the underlying asset. This implies it has two separate strike prices and two different exercise dates.

Compound choices come in four varieties:

Make a phone call

Make a put call

Wear a putty

A phone call

This form of option is more common in the fixed income or currency markets, where there are greater ambiguities about a certain option's ability to protect against risk. The benefits of utilizing a compound option include more leverage at a lower cost. It is vital to remember that the resultant premium will still be higher than the standard choice.

Bermuda options acquire their name from the fact that Bermuda is about halfway between Europe and the United States. Bermuda options may be exercised at the expiry date as well as at various periods before the expiration date. This sort of option is helpful because it gives the writer more control over when the option may be exercised while also giving the buyer a cheaper alternative to the normal American option without any of the European option restrictions. Quantity-Adjusting Options, often known as Quanto options, provide a buyer with access to foreign assets while enabling them to acquire the option in their own native currency. This is an excellent alternative for investors who want to obtain exposure to a new market but do not want to deal with exchange rate fluctuations.

For example, if a French investor is interested in Brazilian options owing to the country's positive economic status, they may invest in the BOVESPA Index, which is the principal stock market in Brazil. To do so without being concerned about the exchange rate between the euro and the Brazilian real, they would acquire a quantity-adjusting call option on the BOVESPA that was denominated in euros. This allows the investor to try to gain money as they normally would without worrying about receiving a dividend that may be reduced owing to unfavorable exchange rates.

Because it is effectively a two-in-one bundle, this option will naturally command a higher price than the norm. This fact gives additional premiums to authors of quantity-adjusting options in addition to the increased risk they face when dealing with exchange rates, so purchasers do not have to.

Options for looking back: When look-back options are originally formed, they do not have a predetermined price at which they may be exercised. Instead, the holder of these options is free to exercise at any time before the option expires at the most advantageous price. These options eliminate all of the risk involved with correctly timing market entrance, making them more costly than regular options kinds.

Assume an investor purchases a call option with the exotic modifier of a 1-month look-back. Once the option matures, the exercise price will be determined by taking the lowest price that the underlying stock ended up attaining over its lifespan. The underlying stock finishes up at $106 at expiry, and the lowest price it ever hit was $71, thus the payment is the difference between $106 and $71, or $35.

Option for a basket: A basket option is identical to a vanilla option, with the distinction that it is based on more than one underlying stock. A basket option, for example, is one that pays out dependent on the price of not just one, but three underlying equities. Each underlying asset may then be valued the same amount in the eventual total, or they can be weighted in a variety of different ways.

CHAPTER 23:

SIMPLIFIED OPTIONS TRADE EXAMPLES

Without the context of a real deal, it may be difficult for a newbie to grasp options trading and the myriad accompanying jargon.

As a result, you'll learn about two separate deals involving a cow breeder and cattle dealers in this section - trades that will help you comprehend the relationship between options trading and actual trading in the real world.

The first transaction is an example of a normal call option trade, while the second is an example of a put option trade.

After reading through these examples, you will understand how to call options and put options function. These examples should also help you understand the different terminologies used in trading.

Bob's Call Option Trade is the first trade.

Jacob is a farmer and cattle breeder with a herd of dairy cows.

Bob, a friend of Jacob's, is a farmer's market dealer.

Bob learns from a friend one day that the town's primary dairy is negotiating a contract with a huge multinational chocolate manufacturing firm. If the contract goes through, the chocolate firm will buy three times as much milk from the dairy every day. To fulfill this increased demand, the dairy would have to expand milk output, which would necessitate the acquisition of a large number of dairy cows on short notice - a move that may result in a significant rise in cow prices locally.

Bob realized he could earn a lot of money if he purchased several cows from Jacob and then sold them when the prices rose.

However, Bob was unsure about this advice and did not want to acquire cows at the full price of $2,000 (the market price for a dairy cow at the time) and then sell at a loss if the price would not increase as projected.

As a result, Bob approaches Jacob and offers him a one-of-a-kind proposition.

Bob informs Jacob that he would pay him $50 in advance for the opportunity to purchase one of his cows at the current market price of $2,000 for the next 30 days. Furthermore, Jacob would be under no duty to refund that sum if Bob no longer wants to exercise his right (if cow prices fell below $2,000

).

Jacob saw no reason for cow prices to rise anytime soon and was happy to accept a contract for $50 from trader Bob in return for granting Bob the right to purchase a cow at $2,000 for the following 30 days.

However, Jacob stipulates that the proposed contract should include 5 cows rather than just 1 cow, which meant that Bob would have to pay a total of $250 for the right to acquire 5 cows for a 30-day period.

Bob agrees to Jacob's requirement, so Jacob takes Bob's $250 and signs the contract, which gives Bob the right (but not the responsibility) to purchase 5 of Jacob's cows for $2,000 during the following 30 days.

Bob recognized that in the following 30 days, the market price of cows would either climb (as he predicted), remain the same, or possibly plummet (in the worst-case scenario).

If the market price for cows remained at $2,000 or went below that level in the following 30 days, Bob would simply have to forfeit the $250 he gave Jacob to secure the deal. Bob was under no obligation to purchase cows at a cheaper price;therefore, his losses will be limited to $250 - the amount he paid Jacob to sign the deal.

If, on the other hand, the market price for cows rose during the following 30 days, Bob would approach Jacob and ask for 5 cows at $2,000 each, and Jacob would be legally obligated to sell the cows at that price, regardless of how much more the cows were worth at the time.

Bob sits and waits.

Three weeks after the contract was signed, the local dairy struck an agreement with the chocolate firm to almost double their daily supply of milk to the chocolate company. To fulfill that demand, the dairy began acquiring a significant number of dairy cows at ever higher costs, causing dairy cow prices in the area to rise by about 25%.

Following the price increase, Bob goes to Jacob and exercises his right to purchase the five cows for $2,000 each. Bob then proceeds to sell these cows to the dairy for $2,500 apiece.

Bob, therefore, receives a total profit of $2,250 for these five cows ($500 times five minus the $250 he paid Jacob for the contract).

The transaction between Bob and Jacob is an example of how an options trade works, and if we apply stock market terminology to the aforementioned situation, then:

One cow symbolizes a single underlying Share/Stock.

Bob is the contract's buyer, while Jacob is the contract's seller. This contract is a Call Option since it offers the buyer the right to purchase.

$2,000 symbolizes the Market Price of the provided company's share (at the time the agreement was signed).

$2,000 also indicates the Strike-Price (SP), or the pre-determined price at which the proposed deal between the buyer (Bob) and the seller (Jacob) would take place - Remember how Jacob paid $50 for a cow with a set price of $2,000?

The Premium is the $50 paid against each cow.

The number 5 denotes the contract's Lot Size, which is the set number of shares that each individual options contract covers.

Finally, the 30 days in this case represent the options contract's Time to Expiry.

I hope you now completely understand how a call option works.

Jacob's Put Option Trade is the second trade.

Jacob begins to consider his options after being forced to sell five of his cows for less than market value owing to a contractual commitment.

Jacob's experience has shown that when cattle prices rise rapidly owing to a change in the environment, the prices ultimately fall somewhat before achieving stability.

However, Jacob wasn't sure whether cow prices had reached their peak yet; if he sold his cows right immediately and prices continued to increase, he'd lose out on an opportunity to sell at even higher rates. The market price for a cow was present at $2,500, and Jacob intended to wait a few weeks to see whether it rose anymore. If prices were already high and then fell drastically, Jacob wanted to be sure he could sell a couple of cows for at least $2,400.

Given his situation, Jacob chooses to enter into a contract identical to the one he previously signed with Bob. He would, however, be the 'buyer' of the right this time - the right to sell cows at a predetermined price (as opposed to the right to buy that Bob acquired from him).

Jacob contacts Chad, a cattle seller in the local market, and offers him a contract for this reason. The agreement stated that Jacob would have the right to sell Chad ten cows at $2,400 apiece for the following 60 days. And Jacob would pay $30 for each cow to acquire that privilege, for a total of $300 for ten cows.

Chad accepts and joins up for the arrangement, pocketing the $300 since he didn't anticipate costs to decrease below $2,400 from $2,500. He had nothing to lose as long as cow prices continued over $2,400 for the following two months (which Chad believed was quite probable).

A month and a half later, Jacob's forecast came true, and cow prices fell to $2,250.

As a result, Jacob travels to Chad and exercises his right to sell the cows for $2,400.

Chad has no alternative but to acquire the cows at the predetermined price since he was legally obligated to do so, despite the fact that the animals are worth $150 less in the market. Jacob profited from his deal by $1200 ($150 x 10 minus the $300 paid for the contract).

Let's apply the numerous stock market terminology to this deal like we did last time:

One cow symbolizes a single underlying Share/Stock.

- Jacob is the contract's Buyer, while Chad is the contract's Seller. This contract is a Put Option because it offers the buyer the right to sell.
- $2,500 - the cost of the cow - symbolizes the current market price of a share (at the time the deal was signed).

- The Strike-Price (SP), or the fixed price at which the proposed exchange between the Buyer (Jacob) and the Seller (Chad), is $2,400.
- The Premium is the $30 paid against each cow.
- The Lot Size of the contract is indicated by the number 10.
- Finally, the 60 days in this case represent the options contract's Time to Expiry.

CHAPTER 24:

WHEN TO ENTER AND EXIT THE TRADE

Did you ever play double Dutch jump rope as a child? Double Dutch is a game in which two persons swing two ropes and a third person must jump in for a few seconds before leaping out. It was painful and tough to find the correct moment to leap in without being smacked with a rope when I was a youngster. Making a deal might be just as nerve-racking. You may be preparing to join the market and stressing yourself out with concerns like, "Do I leap in now? "How about right now?" However, with some strategic preparation and experience, you may locate the ideal sector in which to participate regularly.

The point at which you wish to acquire an asset is the entry point in a transaction. It is the opening bid in your transaction. Whether you're trading stocks or options, you'll always need an entry point.

Having a strong strategy for when you will get into a transaction is really advantageous since it prevents you from driving yourself insane. It also means you won't be making an emotional decision about when to enter.

Selecting a suitable entry position entails inspecting the chart for support, resistance, and trend. Examine the chart's previous movement to identify areas of support and resistance. Then consider the trend. Is the chart following a certain trend line? Or was it in a state of consolidation? Or a time when the market has been somewhat stable? You may select a spot just after a rebound with a stock that has a trend line. Assume stock ABC was trading at $60 in November before falling to $58 in December. As the number begins to increase again, you can observe whether the chart seems to be returning to trend. whether so, you may set your entry point around $60 and wait to see whether the trend continues higher.

When a stock is in neutral movement, your support and resistance lines will be horizontal, and the chart will stay between those two lines. In this situation, repeat the previous movement's pattern and position your entry point at the price where a rebound is expected to occur. This should be along the support line. In this instance, there is a significant likelihood that the stock price will increase again toward the resistance.

Let's get things started. I selected two distinct practice charts. One should have a stock that is moving higher, as well as one that is stable and not heading in a certain way. Draw the trend line at the place of the support line on the one that is heading upward. Choose a posture that gives you a modest swing up from there. When would you get into the swing? What is the pricing point? How long would you keep swinging? Do the same for the chart that is still stable. Where would you enter the trade above the support line? It's simple to accomplish this with previous charts since everything is already in place. However, take the time to examine the chart. What makes some swings more effective and what makes them fail?

Now, attempt a mock futures deal. Find a chart for a stock that you are interested in acquiring. Plan your lines, identify the trading zone, and then choose an entry point in the present or future. After then, keep an eye on the stock for the next several days. Would your deal have worked out? If so, why? And why not, if not? All of this experience allows you to experiment with trades before investing any funds. Once you're comfortable with entrance points, you may move on to departure points.

When you join the trade, make sure that your risk/reward ratio makes the deal worthwhile. After calculating the ratio, you may choose when to leave the transaction in order to make the payoff worthwhile.

Now we'll look at how to exit a transaction. It is critical to have an exit plan. Without an exit plan, you will abandon a trade whenever you feel like it, which may result in losses. You may leave too soon or too late. It is preferable to have a plan in place so that you know precisely when you will depart. For example, if you decide you want to earn a certain amount of money, that is your departure point. Don't go any further.

As you toss it, momentum propels it higher but at a reduced rate until it reaches its maximum. Momentum is zero at this time, and the ball returns to your hands. You want to quit a swing trade before the momentum approaches zero. Not at the summit, but before it. This is because most traders will be aiming to sell at the top of the transaction, causing the market to fall.

It is risky to sell before the predicted peak. It is possible that you may lose if the ball continues to rise significantly higher than expected. However, you will have earned a profit before any reversal occurs, and you can easily buy back into the trend if you like.

When looking at a stock's charts, bear in mind where you want to enter and where you want to leave. If the stock has been stable for some time and is still inside its range, looking at the support and resistance levels might help you decide where to depart. If you entered near the support, you may choose where you want to depart. This is determined by a variety of criteria, including your risk tolerance and length of time in the transaction. In general, if the stock price continues to rise, you should sell before it reaches the resistance level. Remember that in swing trading, it's all about tiny profits, not big ones, thus it's better to leave with some profit than none.

• With your support and resistance lines drawn on a chart, you may search for crucial indications that indicate it's time to sell. One of these indications is if the stock price surpasses its resistance or falls below its support levels. This might indicate that it is beginning to trend in one way, but it could also indicate that these little breakouts will revert to the previous range. whether the stock price surpasses its resistance and you haven't sold yet, you may either wait for it to return to its range or see whether it signals the start of a new trend. This choice, once again, is based on how much risk you are prepared to accept.

There are a few things you can take to ensure that you do not remain in a trade for too long. The first step is to establish a stop-loss. A stop-loss order is a mechanism that will sell your shares if the stock price falls too low. Another alternative is to place a limit order. A limit order will sell your transactions whenever they reach the amount you specify.

Assume ABC's current stock price is $20 per share when you enter. You may place your limit order at $25 per share. You may also configure it to a certain profit percentage. This indicates that your broker will sell your shares at the $25 level. This may be beneficial since it limits your losses, but it can also prevent you from capitalizing on a potential trend. So, once again, make a selection depending on your risk tolerance.

You should ask yourself a few questions as you plan your escape strategy. You should know how long you are willing to remain in a trade, how much risk you are prepared to take, and when you want to exit. These three factors will assist you in developing an effective departure plan.

For example, while deciding how long to remain in a trade, consider how long you want your money to be tied up, what signs you're looking for that will drive you to sell, and so on.

Consider a few distinct possibilities when deciding how much danger you're prepared to accept. Consider what a profit means to you. Is $1 per share a good profit, or do you wish to earn more? Finally, think about when you want to abandon the transaction. This should be properly put down. Are you going to exit the trade after you've gained a particular profit, when you reach the resistance level, or when you notice another sign that it's time to exit? It's critical that you keep to your strategy after you've formed it. This will assist you in being emotionally impartial when trading.

It's time to practice again once you've decided on your departure strategy. Examine some previous charts and consider where you would have entered and left the trade based on indicators such as support and resistance or the moving average. Examine each component of a maneuver.

Why might a certain exit point have succeeded or failed? After that, try it again with a future chart. You may do this in a simulation or on your preferred chart website. Choose a stock to follow and an entry point that you believe will work for you. Then, using your exit plan, decide when to leave the chart. Spend a few days reviewing your strategy as the chart progresses. Did your strategy work? Is there any other way you could have done it? Continue to practice; don't stop at one chart and believe you're ready to trade.

Why and where should you put your stop-loss?

We've discussed stop-losses briefly, but let's go through them in further depth and look at the many varieties available. A stop-loss is analogous to a fire alarm. The fire alarm in your home begins to sound the instant it detects smoke. It does not have to be an actual fire to raise the alarm. This may be annoying, but it is also a near parallel to what a stop-loss is. Yes, a stop-loss may be annoying at times if it is not properly established. When the market takes an unexpected turn, a stop-loss might let you liquidate your trades. It serves as both a warning system and a safety net. It ensures that if the market falls, you will not lose a significant amount of money. However, occasionally a stop-loss is positioned too tightly, causing it to be triggered during normal market volatility. This is the vexing false fire alarm. Even though it is inconvenient, a stop-loss order may save you a lot of trouble. As a swing trader, your transactions will span certain days and weekends, resulting in risky evenings when the market moves suddenly. A stop-loss order may assist you to guarantee that your losses aren't too severe.

CHAPTER 25:

FINANCIAL LEVERAGE

To employ leverage, you must use a variety of products, such as futures, options, and margin accounts. Leverage in options trading might help you increase your earnings. Trading options may provide you with a lot of leverage and enable you to make a lot of money with a modest investment.

Definition

The capacity to trade a high number of options with a little quantity of cash is referred to as leverage. Many traders believe that leverage is dangerous, however, studies have shown that the risk in leveraged options is roughly identical to that of non-leveraged instruments.

What Makes Leverage Riskier?

Trading options with leverage is typically deemed riskier since it exaggerates the business's potential. For example, you may invest $500 to initiate a trade with a potential profit of $7000. Remember the first rule of trading: never trade what you cannot afford to lose.

This isn't as true as it seems, which is why you should always be aware of what you're doing.

Leverage allows you to make better use of your money. As a result, many traders like the trade since it enables them to take on greater holdings with minimal cash.

When you utilize leverage, you are not lowering your potential reward; rather, you are lowering your risk in particular transactions. For example, if you wish to invest in 10,000 options at $8 a share, you will need to risk $80,000 in total. This implies that the whole $80,000 would be in danger. You may, however, utilize leverage to put in a lesser amount of money, lowering your chance of loss.

This is how you should look at leverage, and it is the correct way to look at it.

Before you can trade leverage, you must first figure out how to optimize your profits on each deal.

Here are a few ideas to get you started:

Understand When to Run

You must cut your losses early and then let your winning deals run to a conclusion. Just like in other businesses, you must know when to stop your losses in order to avoid becoming bankrupt. When using leverage in trading, you must apply stop losses.

Do you have a stop loss in place?

As a trader, you must set your stop loss so that you do not lose more than you can afford. The set you create will be determined by the current state of the market. Whatever the circumstance may be, always have a set to guide you.

Don't Make the Trade

Many traders strive to follow a deal all the way to the conclusion, which ends up depressing them and costing them money. Once a move occurs, you must accept it and wait for the next opening. Always be patient, since another chance will undoubtedly present itself, just as the last one did.

Have Order Limits

Instead of putting market limits, use limit orders to save money on commissions. Limit orders can help you control your emotions while trading.

Discover Technical Analysis

Before you begin trading, be sure you understand technical analysis. Technical analysis will ensure that you have the knowledge you need to make quick judgments.

The Benefits of Using Leverage in Options Trading

Leverage allows you to boost your financial potential as a trader and get greater trading outcomes. You have complete control over the amount of leverage. This is because when you create a trading account, you have complete control over the amount of funds you deposit on a transaction. The good news is that you can utilize leverage for free, but you must first understand how it works and if it will work for you.

The degree of leverage varies. Some trading platforms provide leverage ranging from 1:1 to and above 1:1000. As a trader, you should aim for the most leverage feasible in order to maximize your profits.

Another benefit is that minimal leverage helps you to survive as a rookie trader. When you first start trading options, you have the ability to make little deals with nothing to show for your efforts. You may utilize leverage to conduct trades for thousands of dollars without risking the same amount of money in terms of investment. You have the potential to make a big income as long as you know what you're doing.

The Drawbacks of Leverage in Options Trading

As much as it is a terrific approach to produce enormous income, you must also remember that leverage has several drawbacks. These are some examples:

Increases the Losses

With leverage, you will suffer massive losses if the deal goes against you. And since the initial investment is much less than what you end up losing, many traders are unaware that they are putting their cash in danger. Make sure you develop a ratio that will safeguard your interests and then understand how to handle trading risk.

There are no privileges.

When you deal using leverage, you give up complete ownership of the asset. For example, when you employ leverage, you forfeit the ability to get dividends. This is because the payout amount is withdrawn from the account regardless of the trade's status.

Calls for Margin

A margin call occurs when the lender requests more cash to keep the deal open. To limit your exposure, you must determine whether to increase money or abandon a position.

Expenses incurred

When you utilize leverage to trade options, you will obtain funds from the lender in order to employ the whole position. Most traders like to leave their positions open overnight, which incurs a charge to cover the expenditures.

How Much Leverage Do You Need When Trading Options?

Understanding how to trade options requires a thorough understanding of numerous facets of economics. Many people's losses are caused by a lack of awareness about how to employ leverage.

According to research, many traders who use options lose money. This occurs for both low and high leverage.

High Leverage Risks

The capital for making a transaction in options trading is often obtained through a broker. While you may borrow large sums to put on a trade, you can win much more if the deal is successful.

Traders could give leverages of up to 400 times the starting capital only a few years ago. However, limits and limitations have been established, and you may now only access 50 times what you have.

For example, if you have $1,000, you may demand up to $50,000.

Choosing the Appropriate Leverage

When deciding on the kind of leverage that would work best for you, you must consider a number of criteria.

To begin, start with minimal amounts of leverage since the more you borrow, the more you must repay. Second, you must employ stops to ensure that the money borrowed is protected. Remember that losses will not sit well with you.

Overall, you should choose the leverage that is most comfortable for you. If you are a newbie, use modest leverage to reduce dangers. If you know what you're doing, go for maximum leverage to increase your returns.

Using stop orders helps you to limit your losses when the transaction reverses direction. This is the only protection you need as a newcomer to make it in the market. This is due to the fact that you will learn about the trades and how to place them while reducing any losses that may occur.

Risk Management in Options Trading

Options trading has a range of risks that must be managed in order to maximize earnings while minimizing losses.

Here are a few dangers and how to avoid them.

Loss of More Than You Have

This risk is inherent in options trading, particularly when employing leverage to execute a deal. It implies you just put up a little portion of the original investment to start the deal. This implies that the direction of the market determines your destiny. If your forecast is correct, you will profit more than the investment. However, if the trend reverses and you lose the position, you may wind up losing more than your original investment.

When this occurs, you must have a plan in place to assist limit the risk. In this instance, you should create a limit to indicate the precise amount at which the transaction should end so that you don't lose more than you can manage.

Unexpected Position Closings

Positions that shut suddenly result in a loss of money. You must have money in your account to keep the transactions open.

This is known as the margin, and if you do not have enough cash to cover the margin, the position may be closed.

To avoid this, keep an eye on the running balances and constantly increase cash as required.

Sudden Massive Losses or Gains

The market may become turbulent, and when it happens, you must act quickly. Markets fluctuate in response to news or anything else in the market, which might be an announcement, an event, or changes in trading activity.

Aside from having stopped, you should also get alerts about any approaching movement, which informs you whether or not to respond.

Orders filled in incorrectly

When you direct a broker to conduct a deal for you, the broker performs the reverse. This is known as slippage. When this occurs, utilize assured stops to protect yourself from any slippage that may occur.

How to Use Leverage to Trade Smarter

Even with leverage, you need to be able to trade better.

With so many errors made throughout a transaction, you risk losing more than you earn if you don't have the appropriate recommendations to succeed. Let's take a look at the top blunders you make on your way to the top.

Misinterpretation of Leverage

Many newcomers do not comprehend leverage and proceed to abuse it, oblivious to the danger they are subjecting themselves to. Learn about and master leverage to make this work for you.

Learn what it is and what it isn't, and then discover the best ways to utilize it. You must also determine how much you can invest without incurring significant losses.

Having No Exit Strategy

When trading options, you must manage your emotions, just like socks. It doesn't mean you have to swallow your greed and anxiety; rather, you need to have a strategy in place. Once you've made a strategy, you must keep to it so that even when things don't go as planned, you have something to help you recover.

You must have an exit strategy, which implies you must know when to abandon a deal.

Failure to Experiment with New Strategies

Depending on the degree of trading you wish to reach, you should test out a few fresh tactics. Most traders develop a single strategy and adhere to it even when it isn't working.

When this occurs, you are often inclined to break the rules that you have established.

Keep an open mind in order to discover new option trading tactics that will help you get more out of your transactions.

CHAPITRE 26:

MONEY

In options trading, the word moneyness refers to an option's financial state. If the strike price of an option is less than the price of the underlying asset, it is considered to be in the money. It would be profitable, for example, if you could exercise your rights to purchase the underlying stock at the strike price and immediately sell it on the market for a profit.

However, there are other facets to the idea of money.

Remember that the strike price is the fixed price at which the underlying stock may be purchased or sold if the option is exercised. As a result, the strike price is a significant aspect in evaluating the Option's value since we can compare it to the real market price of the stock. This link between the strike price and the actual market price defines the intrinsic value of the Option and will be a deciding factor:

In terms of money: When the striking price and the stock price are the same, this applies to both calls and puts.

Near the cash: Because it is unusual that the strike and real prices would completely match, any approach to equality is referred to be near the money.

In terms of money: When the strike price of a call option is less than the price of the underlying stock. A put option, on the other hand, is in the money when the strike price is greater than the stock price.

Out of pocket: This occurs when the strike price of a call option is greater than the stock price. When the strike price of a put option is less than the stock price, the option is considered out of the money.

You will become extremely acquainted with these words as you begin to practice and acquire expertise dealing with quotation tables and orders.

This is because you will quickly grow used to utilizing the connection between the stock price and the strike price to assess if the Option has any intrinsic value. It's important to remember that only options that are "in the money" have inherent value.

Indeed, an option is considered to be in the money if exercising it is lucrative. If it is not lucrative, it is a loss. This implies that just because the strike price is higher or lower than the real price does not indicate it is in the money since we must constantly include the cost of the premium. Furthermore, the connection between the underlying price and the strike price is determined by the kind of option.

In other words, if the strike price is less than the underlying stock price, the long call is in the money. As a result, you would benefit if you exercised your option rights by purchasing the underlying item and then selling it at a higher market price. If, on the other hand, the underlying stock price is lower than the strike price, the option is worthless.

In contrast, the writer of the option, the trader who is obligated to satisfy the holder's rights, whether to purchase or sell, will have the opposite viewpoint. The writer of the Option has taken a short position and will be out of the money when the underlying asset's price is more than the striking price and, in the money, when the underlying asset's price is less than the exercise price.

Similarly, when we examine the relative views of the put option holder and writer, the positions are inverted. For example, if the holder of a put option has a strike price of $35 and the underlying stock is trading at more than $35, the long put position would be out of the money since exercising would be unprofitable. Long put holders, on the other hand, would be in the money if the underlying traded for less than $35.

However, if we look at the short put position, we can see that an underlying price of greater than $35 means the option will not be executed by the holder, allowing the writer to retain the premium and be in the money. However, if the underlying stock price falls below $35, the option will be in the money from the holder's viewpoint since it may be exercised at a profit, and the writer's short position will be out of the money.

The table below provides a nice overview of everything.

The Profitability of an Option Position Out of the Money in the Money

Position	In the Money	Out of the Money
Long call	Stock>Strike	Stock < Strike
Short call	Stock<Strike	Stock > Strike
Long put	Stock < Strike	Stock > Strike
Short put	Stock > Strike	Stock < Strike

Stock = current market price of the underlying stock(variable)

Strike = the option's locked-in strike price (fixed).

As we can see, the holder and writer of the options are always in opposing positions, unless the strike price and underlying price are the same, in which case the option is at or near the money. This is true regardless of whether the option is a put or a call, or if you are going long or short.

Furthermore, the style of an option has no bearing on its money. This implies that, even though a European option can only be exercised at the expiration time, it may nevertheless transition several times throughout that time, often hopping between being in, out, or at the money at any one moment.

Interest Is Open

A fascinating measure that is often included in quotation tables for Option contracts is a graphical representation of open interest, which is the total number of outstanding options contracts. At the conclusion of each day, open interest is totaled. Open interest is a statistic that is used to gauge market sentiment. It should not be confused with the number of options trading since it is not the same as volume because many options are traded to close out existing holdings.

However, if you are speculating in short-term options trading, Open Interest is a crucial measure since you will want as much market interest on your option as possible. This will make trading simpler when you decide to exit the position since there will most likely be many possible buyers.

Options expire at regular intervals indicated by the expiry date, which is the day the option expires. The majority of options expire on the third Friday of each month. Some high-volume weekly options, on the other hand, have expiry dates every Friday. The option may be traded until the market closes shortly before the option expires.

Some European options shut early (occasionally on a Thursday, although the closing time is mentioned for the option, and most broker applications check the expiration dates of options and give a message, so you'd know):

The option period is the word used to designate the time until expiration that begins when the option is created (written) and ends on the expiry day. However, there are methods to extend your employment beyond the expiration date. If you wish to keep the position, you may roll it by closing your existing - soon-to-expire - open position and opening a new one with a different strike price or expiry date.

Weighing the Costs and Benefits of Alternatives

There are several advantages to trading options, but you won't gain all of them unless you accept some level of risk.

One significant risk that you must understand is that options have a limited lifetime due to their expiration date. When dealing with this risk, you must have clear plans in place, such as an exit strategy. For example, you might trade the option within its time period, let it expire on or before the expiration date, or just let it expire.

However, just allowing choices to expire might be a major issue. For example, if the option is in the money at expiry, your broker may exercise/assign the option automatically. The issue here is that they have essentially transformed a low-cost option position into a high-cost stock position, which you may not desire or be able to afford by exercising the valued option. As a result, you must closely watch your options and look for warnings from the broker platform about any in-the-money option contracts that are about to expire. You must do this in advance of the expected change in your margin need.

Alternatively, you should ensure that you have enough time to sell the option or make other modifications, such as rolling over a transaction, to avoid purchasing the stock.

Leverage Risk

Another important issue to be aware of is leverage. Because options are a contract rather than a stock, they enjoy disproportionately bigger percentage price gains in response to the significantly more costly underlying stock's relatively minor price fluctuations. The great advantage of this is that it produces big percentage returns even if the underlying stock moves by a tiny amount in the expected direction. The disadvantage is that it leads to a complete loss of investment if the stock moves even a tiny amount in the incorrect direction. This isn't generally a worry for novices, or at least it shouldn't be since the risk presents itself mostly by trading with too big a position size. However, you should be aware that, although leverage is plainly useful, it can also be a double-edged sword, so be aware that leverage is a danger that must be managed. One easy method to eliminate or reduce this amount of risk is to keep your position size minimal.

Finally, as we know, options have a temporal value (extrinsic value) in addition to their underlying intrinsic value (in the money value), which is a double-edged sword. Time decay operates as a headwind for option purchasers since it constantly reduces the option's value. This raises the need for bigger stock price movements to break even on the deal. It operates as a tailwind for option writers since it permits a profit to be produced via consistent premium revenue regardless of whether the stock moves or not.

Two additional cost variables for alternative options should be considered:

- Costs related to the trading process
- The price of exercising the stock

Understanding the fundamental cost structure of an option allows you to grasp how options, although providing leverage at a lower risk, add an element of risk via leverage.

To make matters more complicated, option pricing is partly dependent on probability. Given the price changes of the underlying stock lately, you should analyze the possibility that a certain option will be in-the-money before or at expiry.

The valuation of an option considers six factors: stock price, strike price, time to expiry, interest rates, and dividends, but there is one wildcard factor: volatility.

Conclusion

Setting up passive income streams is one of the most popular approaches to achieving financial independence. Options trading has the potential to be a lucrative kind of passive income. This activity not only provides the trader with a platform to obtain financial independence, but also enables the trader to pursue hobbies, job alternatives, and other activities that he or she enjoys. This is possible since the trader is not actively exchanging time for money. Options traders have the freedom to live and work anywhere in the globe since, when done correctly, trading options enables the trader to make tens of thousands of dollars or more while sleeping.

This book was written as a comprehensive guide to demonstrate that anyone can earn a substantial income from options trading as long as they are willing to develop a growth mindset, learn from the mistakes and successes of other traders, and work to make that initial human and financial investment. Options are derivative contracts that provide the contract owner the right to purchase or sell the related asset by a defined expiry date. This term indicates that this is not something you should dabble with every now and then.

Are You Prepared to Become an Option Trader?

Options trading is a business. As a result, it must be treated with a mentality geared toward growth and progress. We've covered a variety of subjects on how to get started, including creating a training plan, paper trading, obtaining a brokerage account, and deciding on a trading style. As a newcomer in this industry, all of these elements, as well as mastering the terminology of options trading, are critical. Without that first research, you will not be able to advance in your job and earn as much as you would want.

After that, you must actually use the concepts and tactics presented in this book. You must be able to watch a put option and a call option in action in order to remember what they are. To psychologically establish what a long and short posture is, you must physically be in these positions. To get acquainted with volatility and interest rates, you must first place yourself in a position to learn more. Straddles, strangles, legging, debit spreads, credit spreads, naked option sales, and option rolling... They may seem daunting on paper and may be tough to apply at first, but practice makes perfect. Every expert options trader began as a novice, but constant, relentless work propelled them to the next level.

This is a new world for any rookie, and it may be scary, but if you stay devoted to developing the attributes of a great options trader, you will be well on your way to achieving the financial independence that you want. There will be setbacks and failures, as with any new enterprise. You will sometimes lose your footing and be exposed to things you have never been exposed to before.